WORSHIP IN TRANSITION

WORSHIP IN TRANSITION

The Liturgical Movement in the Twentieth Century

John R. K. Fenwick
and Bryan D. Spinks

CONTINUUM • NEW YORK

1995
The Continuum Publishing Company
370 Lexington Avenue, New York, NY 10017

This edition published under license from T&T Clark Ltd

Printed in Great Britain

Library of Congress Cataloging-in-Publication Data

Fenwick, John R. K., 1951–
Worship in transition : the liturgical movement in the twentieth century / John R. K. Fenwick and Bryan D. Spinks.
p. cm.
Includes bibliographical references and index.
ISBN 0-8264-0827-3 (pbk. : alk. paper)
1. Liturgical movement—Catholic Church—History. 2. Liturgical movement—Protestant churches—History. I. Spinks, Bryan D.
II. Title.
BV182.F46 1995
264'.009'04—dc20 95-8724
CIP

Typeset by Waverley Typesetters, Galashiels
Printed and bound in Great Britain by Page Bros, Norwich

Contents

FOREWORD vii

1. *Introduction* 1
2. *Characteristics of the Liturgical Movement* 5
3. *Pre-1900 Forerunners to the Liturgical Movement* 13
4. *Rediscovery, Research and Renewal: The Roman Catholic Liturgical Movement 1900–62* 23
5. *The Anglican Church and the Liturgical Movement I* 37
6. *South Indian Springboard* 53
7. *The Roman Catholic Church: From Vatican II to the New Roman Rites 1963–90* 61
8. *The Anglican Church and the Liturgical Movement II* 71
9. *The Liturgical Movement in the English Reformed and Methodist Churches* 81
10. *The Eastern Churches and the Liturgical Movement* 95
11. *The Impact of the Charismatic Movement* 105
12. *Behind the Consensus on the Eucharist* 115
13. *The Changing Face of Baptism and Confirmation* 135
14. *The Language of Worship* 147

15. *Inculturation* 157

16. *Opposition and Reaction* 167

17. *The Daily Office, Pastoral Offices and Ordination: Highlights and Questions* 175

18. *Snapshots of the Movement in North America* 187

19. *Where Next?* 195

INDEX 199

Foreword

As long ago as 1960 the American liturgist Massey Shepherd wrote, 'There is no individual who is competent to give sufficient account of the liturgical renewal in our times.'[1] The authors of this present work would wholeheartedly agree with Shepherd and certainly do not claim to have written 'a sufficient account' of the movement which has transformed the worshipping experience of millions of people in the twentieth century. This is not, then, a definitive history of the Liturgical Movement. However, in our teaching ministries we have identified a need for a more modest work which would bring together between two covers the diverse phenomena which characterize the movement – Guéranger and John Wimber, de Candole and Lefebvre, Gregorian chant and singing in the Spirit, Solesmes and West Africa, Pius X and inclusive language and so on.

In compiling our material we have had to be selective. Each Church, each country, has its own particular experience of the Liturgical Movement and it has not been possible to chart them all. Individual liturgists and historians differ in their assessment of the value of particular contributions, making a definitive selection extremely difficult. Our own identity as presbyters of the Church of England is no doubt to some extent reflected in the examples we have chosen,

[1] M. H. Shepherd, *The Liturgical Renewal of the Church*, New York, OUP, 1960, p. 21.

but we hope that the range of Churches and issues covered will make the book useful in many different situations.

The earlier chapters deliberately concentrate in rather more detail on specific individuals or sequences of events. Indeed, at times they are anecdotal. This is because at this period in particular the progress of the Liturgical Movement was very much bound up with the life and careers of a relatively small number of key individuals. Broader brush strokes are inevitable for describing the later proliferation of the movement and its implications.

We wish to record our indebtedness to Arthur Couratin, Geoffrey Cuming, Colin Buchanan and Ronald Jasper, who introduced us to, and encouraged us in, the study of liturgy; to successive generations of students at Trinity College, Bristol, and the Divinity Faculty, Cambridge, who have helped to refine many of these chapters; and to the many congregations around the world with whom over the years we have been caught up in worship as members of the People of God.

JOHN FENWICK
The Rectory
Chorley
Lancashire

BRYAN SPINKS
Churchill College
Cambridge

1
Introduction

What *is* the Liturgical Movement? Perhaps the most succinct answer is that given in *A New Dictionary of Liturgy and Worship*: 'part of the reawakening of the Church'.[1] The twentieth century has seen the Christian Church worldwide face great challenges and changes. For much of the century large sections of the Church have lived under hostile, atheistic regimes. The experience is said to have produced more martyrs than in all the preceding centuries. Even where persecution has not been so overt, the Church has still suffered a powerful onslaught. Nineteenth-century philosophies, which had no place for God, have been allowed full rein in twentieth-century societies, aided by the effects of two World Wars and numerous local conflicts. In Europe and North America the de-Christianizing of society has been rapid. Practising (i.e. worshipping) Christians now represent only a small proportion of the population. Traditional Christian beliefs, values and morality are now widely abandoned or questioned, even within parts of the Church itself. Only perhaps in Africa has the Church made significant and sustained growth during the last century.

Yet the same period that has witnessed such apparent decline and loss of confidence has also seen 'an extraordinary recovery and renewal by the Christian Church of its worship and the understanding of that worship as central

[1] J. G. Davies (ed.), *A New Dictionary of Liturgy and Worship*, London, SCM Press, 2nd edn., 1986, p. 314.

to its life and work'.[2] It would be wrong to overemphasize the changes. The sacraments, for example, are still recognizably the sacraments, hymn-books are still hymn-books. But equally, it would be foolish to pretend that there have not been vast shifts in the dynamics and expectations of worshipping Christians, often expressed in changed texts, styles, concepts and even buildings. It is these shifts which constitute the Liturgical Movement.

The very name 'Liturgical Movement' is itself misleading in that it suggests a concern solely with written liturgies. This is only partly true. Not only has the movement affected Churches which do not use an official text, but it is also about changing the way Christians think about worship, the expectations they have of it (and of each other), and, indeed, about changing their spirituality. Caught up in the movement is the very way people understand their Christian identity and its expression. Clearly the relationship between this and the forms of worship is a complex one. Often changing understandings have required a change in the texts. Even harder to quantify is the way in which new liturgies have brought about changed perceptions in those using them. If worship is indeed the central activity of the Church it could be argued that all twentieth-century church history should be seen as an outworking of the Liturgical Movement. Such a claim would not go unchallenged. It could be argued, conversely, that the visible changes conveniently described as the Liturgical Movement are themselves merely the tangible results of developments in the world Church which are more conveniently analysed in other categories. No definitive answer is offered here. The chapters which follow simply seek to provide some of the data for exploring the place of the Liturgical Movement within its context.

Movements, perhaps by definition, are made up of many strands. They also illustrate in various ways the relationship

[2] Ibid., p. 307.

between the individual and the corporate. The leader's vision can only become reality if it strikes a chord and elicits a response in others. The Liturgical Movement has certainly had its prophets, visionaries, teachers and leaders. The specific contribution of some of these is detailed here. It is not suggested that the relatively small sample chosen is exhaustive. The names of many others would deserve mention in a definitive history. Here, the intention has been to give a representative selection and to illustrate the ways in which the concepts of the movement spread and found expression. A broader overview, systematizing the main features of the Liturgical Movement, is given in Chapter 2.

Who does the Liturgical Movement belong to? Thanks to the Ecumenical Movement which has accompanied the Liturgical Movement throughout this century, the question can be asked in a non-polemical way. But it remains true that the different branches of the world Church could claim the movement as their own. It can be described as being in genesis and outworking a force within the Roman Catholic Church which has had a knock-on effect in other Churches. Equally, Churches of the Reformation can claim it as a further outworking of their own basic principles. It would not be far-fetched for the Orthodox to describe it as a rediscovery by the other Churches of insights and practices which they have preserved down the centuries. Within the limitations of the present work it can be demonstrated that there is truth in all these claims. Chapters 3, 4 and 7 describe the movement as it has developed in the Roman Catholic Church. Chapters 5 and 8 show how its insights have found expression throughout the worldwide Anglican Communion, while Chapter 9 explores the Methodist and Reformed traditions. The significance of the Orthodox contribution is assessed in Chapter 10. It could well be that the success of the Liturgical Movement is due in large measure precisely to the fact that it has found a resonance within the main families of Christendom.

The ecumenical dimension has also had a profound effect in the realm of liturgical scholarship. Chapters 12, 13 and 17 show how all the traditions have wrestled with the challenge of expressing biblical and historical insights in contemporary practice. While some research is clearly intended to show the rightness of a particular Church's stance, most of it, especially as the century has progressed, is 'pure' in the sense that the results are presented for the different Churches to assess and assimilate. Frequently the results challenge all traditions equally.

Change in the twentieth century has not, of course, been confined to the Church. Profound political, demographic, scientific and social shifts have shaped what is now termed 'the global village'. Some of these are paralleled in the Church. This, of course, raises profound questions about the relationship between the Church and the world in which it is set. How many of the changes in the Church have simply been a following of secular developments? Should the Church and its worship reflect the local culture or challenge it? Some of these issues are raised in Chapters 14, 15 and 16.

Finally, where is the hand of God in all this? Chapter 11 explores the spiritual renewal known as the Charismatic Movement which has greatly influenced the spirituality of millions of Christians in the present century. Is this where God is leading the Church? As that movement itself matures beyond its first enthusiasms the answer to the question becomes more complex. The Liturgical Movement has, arguably, transformed the worshipping life of more Christians than the Charismatic Movement. Both have their limitations and imperfections. Perhaps the two are simply two aspects of a single work of God in this century, a work whose aim is nothing less than 'the reawakening of the Church'.

2

Characteristics of the Liturgical Movement

The chapters which follow will span over a century of history and a wide range of countries and individuals. The purpose of the present chapter is therefore to give an overview of the main features of the movement so that the reader is alerted to what to look out for amidst the details of the broadly historical accounts which follow:

'The struggle for community'[1]

An important strand in the Liturgical Movement is a protest against individualism:

1. *In society.* The modern urban conditions created by the industrial revolution and its aftermath have led to the disintegration of families and communities. Much of the world's population no longer lives in traditional communities where time-honoured relationships provide a framework for living. Philosophically it could be argued that such atomization is the logical outworking of Renaissance individualism. In such a situation the role of the Church as one's true family becomes increasingly important.

2. *In the Church.* Within Roman Catholicism the Mass was no longer a community action, a situation which was strongly defended. The mystical tradition provided a rationale for the people's lack of participation in the rite.

[1] Koenker, *Liturgical Renaissance*, p. 32.

> The main concern was now the soul's union with Christ. Most other Churches were similar. This tended to foster a 'language laboratory' approach to public worship, with no interaction between worshippers. What mattered in an act of worship was that each individual's 'spiritual temperature' was raised.

Theologically, the Liturgical Movement's reaction to this state of affairs has been undergirded by a rediscovery of the New Testament image of the Church as the Body of Christ. The Liturgical Movement has attempted to incarnate this locally by turning congregations into communities (with its implications for local decision-making about worship styles and the quality of community life) and supra-locally with, in episcopal Churches, a new stress on the liturgical expression of the relationship between the bishop and his presbyters and people. The bishop is seen once again as the chief liturgical functionary.

Participation

There has been a reaction against the clericalism of Rome and of most of Protestantism. Also, in Western Europe and North America first, but increasingly in other parts of the world, the proportion of educated, literate worshippers has increased, leading to a new emphasis on *understanding* and involvement. (Parallels can perhaps be seen in management and education styles.) This has resulted in a *decentralizing* of the manner in which worship is conducted. Worship is no longer a spectacle but a community action – a shift which leads to a discovery of the potentially cohesive power of ritual and ceremony.

There have been implications for when worship takes place. Churches have changed worship patterns to accommodate people's needs. For example, since 1953 evening Masses have been permitted in the Roman Catholic Church. Initially the intention was to make it easier for shiftworkers, bakers and those required to work 'unsociable hours' to attend. The permission has been widely used by others, including attending Saturday evening Masses to fulfil Sunday obligations. A second major participatory development has been the presence and involvement of children. This in turn has had repercussions for initiation and eucharistic practice.

Changing concepts of participation have had implications for the dynamics of worship. This has affected both the layout of worship space (architecture, art, furnishings, etc.) and the relationship between ministers and people ('presidents' in the 'westward position': eye contact). There is often a new ethos. Furthermore, heightened awareness by the laity demands new styles and skills from the clergy.

A rediscovery of the early Church as a model

This is not antiquarianism in the sense of 'escaping' to a supposed golden age (though there has been some of that), but an attempt to get back to 'purer' traditions, before medieval and Reformation developments. The intention has not been to *repeat*, but to rediscover certain principles of worship that had been forgotten or overlaid. 'The practice of the undivided Church' still has a powerful appeal. The search for early Church usage feeds on and encourages liturgical research and scholarship. The results make it possible to see current developments and practices in perspective. They also reveal apparent inadequacies (for example, the lack of an epiclesis in Western rites). Lost emphases (for example, thanksgiving as the core of the eucharistic prayer) have been rediscovered. The search for liturgical roots invariably leads to common patterns emerging.

A rediscovery of the Bible

This has been a wider application of a Reformation principle.

1. *Liturgically* – the Liturgy of the Word has been recognized as an essential part of the eucharist. There is a wider

and more systematic use of the Bible (Old Testament lections in the eucharist, the Roman Catholic office lectionary revised, etc.).

2. *Theologically* – A greater range of scriptural concepts and emphases has been incorporated (for example, more stress on the work of the Holy Spirit). Liturgical preaching – linking Christocentric emphasis to the liturgical context – has emerged. (As a result there has been less moral or dogmatic preaching in the Roman Catholic Church). The intention is to let Scripture mould the local community. There is a concern that a fuller range of scriptural themes be reflected in the Church's worship.

A rediscovery of the eucharist

1. Most Reformation Churches (Anglicans included) had infrequent communion. The Liturgical Movement emphasized the concept of 'the Lord's people round the Lord's Table on the Lord's Day' – which has made and continues to make rapid progress. It is now widely recognized as an ideal even in those Churches that have not achieved it (e.g. Methodism).

2. Roman Catholicism and Orthodoxy always had eucharist-centred worship, but with no general communion. Now for Roman Catholics communion began to take place within the eucharist (not as a private devotional exercise before or after it) and was accepted as the norm. This led to calls for the restoration of the cup to the laity, which is now widespread. A rediscovery of the *meal* dimension has become common to most traditions.

An emphasis on the vernacular

1. Within the Roman Catholic Church, as late as 1885, translation of the Missal into the vernacular was forbidden (though many unofficial translations existed). Virtually all services were in Latin (though the Uniat Churches used

the liturgical vernacular). As the Liturgical Movement got under way it soon became apparent that comprehension and involvement require the vernacular.

2. By 1900 the liturgical vernacular in Anglican and Protestant worship was usually archaic in style, even in extempore prayer. Revision was to raise questions as to what form of vernacular should be used.

The shift to modern vernacular has implications for music. New texts often require new settings. They also call for new styles.

The rediscovery of other Christian traditions

Not all individuals involved in the Liturgical Movement are ecumenically aware. Some Roman Catholics and Orthodox, for example, would insist that all that is needed for revision can already be found in their own traditions – there is therefore no need to import ideas from elsewhere. Some Charismatics and Protestants would wish to make their reading of the Bible the sole source. But generally there is a growing awareness of each other and a willingness to learn from each other.

1. This is seen in the world of scholarship, with liturgists of different traditions working on the same ancient sources, reading each other's articles, and attending conferences together. This has resulted in much cross-fertilization.

2. Creators of liturgy (commissions and individuals) now openly borrow good ideas from each other (sometimes to the dismay of some of their constituency).

3. Particularly important has been an awareness of Orthodox traditions for Protestants and Romans. Anglicans led the field (from the eighteenth century), but Rome set up a Pontifical Institute for Oriental Studies in 1917. Orthodoxy preserves many characteristics of early liturgy – deacons, vernacular, congregational participa-

tion, liturgical bishops, etc. Orthodoxy has also retained the concept and reality of worship as *mysterium* – an incarnation of the heavenlies – an emphasis lost in most Western rites. The Roman Catholic Church recognizes the orders and sacraments of Orthodoxy. Re-learning things from the Orthodox is therefore less 'embarrassing' than doing so from Protestants. 'Certain aspects of the oriental rites make a good liturgist of the Roman rite green with envy.'[2] Protestants can see in the East 'catholic' and primitive features free from the taint of medieval Romanism, and therefore easier to borrow than from that source.

4. Especially since Vatican II there has been much co-operation between Roman Catholics and others – e.g. joint work on ICEL, ICET, etc. (see Chapters 7 and 8 for these bodies).

The result is a remarkable degree of similarity between once widely-different traditions, and the pleasant discovery of the familiar in each other's worship.

An emphasis on proclamation and social involvement

True worship and sacramental participation should restore humanity to its true status in Christ, and this should have a visible outworking in society. Increased participation emphasizes the differences between 'insiders' and 'outsiders'. Such a differentiation should be a positive spur to intercession, witness and caring. Worship should therefore be the central activity from which all other activities flow out: 'Send us out in the power of your Spirit . . .' It has been increasingly recognized that the goal of worship is not the indulgence of the worshippers but the transformation of the world. In the 1950s and 1960s there were experiments with worker priests saying Mass on their factory benches. The

[2] Koenker, p. 191.

mood was typified by the inauguration of the Feast of St Joseph the Worker. As the century has progressed the emphasis has shifted to create a Christianly educated and aware laity who recognize their obligation to be evangelistically, politically, economically and ecologically active as a result of their Christian commitment. That commitment is to be fed, focused and informed in worship.

Summary

At its best the Liturgical Movement is about renewing the whole Church, hence the impossibility of describing it adequately. By creating worship that is 'authentic' and that enables a full-orbed exposure to the transforming power of Christ in the Spirit, the people of God are to be motivated and equipped to serve him in the world. The following chapters will attempt to chart and assess to what extent this has been the case.

Selected Reading

P. F. Bradshaw and B. D. Spinks (eds), *Liturgy in Dialogue*, London, SPCK, 1994.

H. Ellsworth Chandlee, 'The Liturgical Movement' in J. G. Davies (ed.), *A New Dictionary of Liturgy and Worship*, London, SCM Press, 2nd edn., 1986.

W. H. Frere, *Some Principles of Liturgical Reform*, London, John Murray, 1911.

D. Gray, *Earth and Altar*, Norwich, Alcuin Club/Canterbury Press, 1986.

E. B. Koenker, *The Liturgical Renaissance in the Roman Catholic Church*, Chicago, University of Chicago Press, 1954.

M. H. Shepherd, *The Liturgical Renewal of the Church*, New York, OUP, 1960.

J. H. Srawley, *The Liturgical Movement*, Alcuin Club Tract 27, London, Mowbray, 1954.

M. Thurian, 'The Present Aims of the Liturgical Movement', in *Studia Liturgica*, 3, 1964, pp. 107–15.

3

Pre-1900 Forerunners to the Liturgical Movement

For most movements there is an event that is conveniently described as their 'beginning'. The Liturgical Movement is no exception. Its starting point is usually identified either as Lambert Beauduin's address to the Malines Conference in 1909, or the publication of his *La Piété de l'Eglise* in 1914. However, the closer one looks at such dates or events, the more arbitrary they seem. Beauduin himself was a product of earlier influences. Others before him had prepared the ground and contributed to the formation of the vision that he articulated and which was to inspire the future course of the Liturgical Movement. The precise significance of each of the earlier influences varies greatly: some are climates of thought that affected whole generations, others are specialist scholars whose immediate contribution was restricted to a narrow field of study but who provided much of the raw material for later liturgical reconstruction. All of them have their place.

The Maurists

Beauduin is a convenient watershed in the history of the Liturgical Movement because while *after* him the movement had a predominantly *pastoral* emphasis, prior to his work the emphasis had been largely *monastic*. Of these monastic forerunners, some of the most prominent were the Maurists. These were Benedictine monks of the Congregation of St Maur in France which was founded in 1621. From 1672 onwards they devoted themselves mainly to historical and literary works, including liturgical texts. Among the most famous of them was Edmond Martène (1654–1707) who compiled a collection of early liturgies: *De Antiquis Ecclesiae Ritibus* (3 volumes 1700–02). Martène himself had trained at the Maurist house at St-Germain-des-Prés under Jean Mabillon (1632–1707) who began to put palaeographic research on a scientific footing. Monks like Mabillon (whose edition of the *Ordines Romani* remained the standard text until the twentieth century) and Montfaucon did much to establish an accepted methodology of consulting a range of manuscripts, collating variant readings, tracing the manuscript history, and so on. 'The Maurist school of scholarship proved a turning point in the inauguration of modern philological and historical method by attempting to achieve a complete accounting of all the material available.'[1] Their work challenged contemporary assumptions by showing many of the features of Roman Catholic worship (for example, confession and the offertory) to be no older than the Middle Ages, and then only modelled on *Roman* use, which had originally been only one among many. Maurist scholars also maintained, on the basis of their research, that expressions of popular theology and piety (which formed the basis of much lay Roman Catholic practice) should not be part of the official liturgical provision.

The pioneering work of the Maurists was brought to an end by the French Revolution and Napoleonic Wars, which resulted in the widespread closure of churches and religious houses in France, Spain, Belgium and Germany. The Maurist Congregation was suppressed in 1790 following the French Revolution, and in 1792 the last Superior General was guillotined with forty of his monks. The Congregation was finally dissolved by Pius VII in 1818.

[1] F. X. Murphy, in *New Catholic Encyclopedia*, Washington, Catholic University of America, Vol. 9, p. 509.

Jansenism

This was a rigorist Augustinian religious movement which caused great turmoil in the sixteenth and seventeenth centuries, especially in the Low Countries. Its name derives from that of Cornelius Jansen, Professor of Theology at Louvain and eventually Bishop of Ypres, who died in 1638. His book *Augustinus* was published posthumously in 1640 and its teaching on grace was fiercely attacked by the Jesuits. The course of the dispute need not concern us here as there is probably no direct causal link with the beginnings of the Liturgical Movement. What is significant, however, is that the Jansenist 'programme' eventually contained a number of items concerned with worship which present interesting parallels with twentieth-century developments.

Jansenist principles included a return to the Bible, an emphasis on early Church usage and the early Fathers, and a desire for the vernacular. Leading figures accused of being associated with the movement, such as Jubé, the parish priest at Asnières near Paris, had only one altar in church and Mass was celebrated only on Sundays and saints' days (i.e. not daily). Outside Mass the altar was bare and even during Mass there were no candles or cross. The people were encouraged to participate by saying the responses. The canon was spoken aloud and the celebrant's chair stood to one side for the Liturgy of the Word.

Some of the above features were set out by the Jansenist Synod of Pistoia (1786) which was condemned by Pius VI in the Bull *Auctorem Fidei* in 1794. As well as condemning the arrogation to itself by a local church of the papal right to make liturgical reforms, the Bull specifically denounced the above practices as well as the assertion that receiving communion was an essential part of the Mass. In all this it has to be acknowledged however that an anti-Roman *political* agenda was involved and no doubt contributed to the violence of papal reactions. (The Archbishopric of Utrecht which was at the centre of the Jansenist controversy was to become in due course the senior of the Old Catholic Churches.)

The Enlightenment

The movement of ideas conventionally known as the Enlightenment blossomed in eighteenth-century Europe, building on the discovery of 'scientific' methodology by Isaac Newton and others in the previous century. It radically altered intellectual thinking and, ultimately, popular assumptions. Two of its broad characteristics are of relevance to the development of the Liturgical Movement:

1. The questioning of received practice. The Enlightenment brought a spirit of enquiry: 'Why are things the way they are?' The answer 'Because they always have been' was no longer sufficient. Old authorities came under examination and criticism. Christianity and its worship did not escape. Pressure for the use of the vernacular was one early result, producing translations of the Missal and Breviary and, in Germany, the *Betsingmesse* where German rather than Latin chants were sung by the people.
2. A move away from an earlier theocentric emphasis to a more human-centred approach to life and the world. Humankind moved to the centre of study previously occupied by God. In other words, questions were asked about *people* and their needs. Positively, this led to a new awareness of the congregation and the human dimension in worship. Negatively, it could be accused of leading to a consumer-orientated approach to worship.

Romanticism

This climate of thinking was in part a reaction to the increasingly destructive effects of the Enlightenment, to the 'dryness' of much eighteenth-century thought and worship, and to the devastation caused by the Napoleonic Wars. (There are some interesting parallels in the late twentieth-century New Age Movement.) Romantics saw the Middle Ages as the great age of faith and piety, with the result that what was done then came to be accepted (often uncritically) as the model for what ought to be done now. Romantic assumptions influenced developments both on the European continent and in Britain. In the latter case, the Oxford Movement, with its increasing emphasis on pre-Reformation practices and architectures, could be said to owe much to Romanticism.

A characteristic feature of the movement on the Continent was the re-opening of religious houses that had been suppressed or destroyed in the aftermath of the French Revolution. This was to have a significant effect on the development of the Liturgical Movement and deserves further comment. The devastation caused to the Church on the Continent is a result of the Revolution frequently overlooked in subsequent accounts. Clearly, a great deal of damage was done and continuities brought to an end (Cluny, for example, was destroyed, never to be rebuilt in its former glory). At the same time the situation created new opportunities. Vacated premises were available to be re-occupied by a new generation of religious, some of them (as will be shown below) with an interest in liturgical scholarship. The new situation also allowed the development of new 'congregations'. It is a feature of Roman Catholic monasticism that within the Orders (e.g. the Benedictines) there are various families or groupings of houses. Often these will have derived from a particular monastery which then becomes the mother house of the 'family' or congregation founded from it. The members of the congregation usually share something of the particular character and specialisms of the mother house. Such congregations were to form important networks through which the ideas of the Liturgical Movement spread. In the early stages, it was the monasteries which were to be the centres and seedbed of the movement.

Prosper Louis Pascal Guéranger (1805–75)

Guéranger vies with Beauduin for the title 'Father of the Liturgical Movement'. He was born at Sable-sur-Sarthe in France and while training for the priesthood became interested in liturgy and the Fathers. He was ordained priest in the Diocese of Le Mans in October 1827. Guéranger had a longing to re-establish the Benedictine Order in France and to enrich both monasticism and liturgical worship by uniting them. In this he was supported by his bishop. In 1833 to further his aim he bought with the help of some friends the deserted priory of Solesmes (whose original foundation had been in 1010) in the Sarthe district. He settled there with five other priests and began to live strictly according to the Rule of St Benedict.

In July 1837 Guéranger was professed as a Benedictine monk at Rome and in September of that year Pope Gregory XVI constituted Solesmes an Abbey (i.e. an official part of the Benedictine Order), with Guéranger as its first abbot. He remained there all his life. The Abbey with its special emphasis attracted monks and gradually became a centre for liturgical exploration and writing, the overall aim being the restoration of the Church's heritage.

One of the main areas of interest at Solesmes was Gregorian chant. From the later Middle Ages this ancient monophonic way of singing was gradually widely displaced by various polyphonic styles and settings. Among Guéranger's monks music scholars like Dom Pothier and, a generation later, Dom Mocquereau studied ancient manuscripts and early chants. Many of the chants were revived in the worship of the community and from there began to spread to the wider Church. This, in Shepherd's opinion, constitutes the glory of Solesmes' work.[2]

Guéranger was a voluminous writer – 126 works are credited to him. He wrote in a popular style and his works were widely circulated. Between 1841 and 1866 he published six volumes of *L'Année Liturgique*, a highly influential devotional commentary on the ecclesiastical year (a further three volumes were written by others after his death). The years 1840–51 saw the appearance of *Institutions Liturgiques*

[2] Shepherd, *Liturgical Renewal*, p. 25.

in three volumes, setting out the principles of liturgical worship.

The positive contributions of Guéranger and his colleagues may be summed up thus:

1. They stimulated scientific liturgical research and prepared the way for subsequent generations of Benedictine liturgical scholars (e.g. Coqin, Cabrol, Battifol and Engberding).

2. They began the dissemination of an interest in the liturgy in the Roman Catholic Church.

3. They stimulated a concern for the correct performance of the liturgy.

Criticisms can, however, be made:

1. Guéranger's scholarship was, initially at least, weak and lacked a critical discipline. In spite of earlier Maurist work, critical textual scholarship was still in its infancy.

2. Like most of his generation (of Romantics) Guéranger looked almost exclusively to the Middle Ages for his interpretation and model. Shepherd describes the problem and the result thus: '[he] was more at home in the piety of the Middle Ages than in that of the Patristic age – and everyone knows, of course, that the medieval period was one of liturgical deterioration.'[3]

3. Guéranger was excessively ultramontane and believed in rigid uniformity to such an extent that he actually contributed to the suppression of some ancient local usages in favour of the strict Roman use.

4. There was little or no social or pastoral concern but, rather, a tendency to an antiquarian or archaeological approach. 'The modern Roman Catholic Liturgical Movement is much more than a concern for the proper rendition of the chant', was Koenker's criticism of this defect in Guéranger's work.[4]

[3] Ibid., p. 24.

[4] Koenker, *Liturgical Renaissance*, pp. 10f.

5. Guéranger was only moderately interested in vernacular liturgy and certainly did not believe that everything should be translated. His comments betray an attitude of superiority:

> Such is the majesty of the liturgical books that they must be safeguarded from the familiarity of the vulgar, both by the sacred language in which they are written, by the mysterious silence at the altar at the most sublime moments, and by the extreme reserve to which one ought to subject translations of the forms of which they are composed.[5]

Despite such criticisms, Guéranger has earned tributes from later generations: 'Dom Guéranger laid such foundations that without his pioneering the work of twentieth-century reformers would be impossible.'[6]

The Beuronese Congregation

This network of Benedictine houses illustrates something of the process by which the ideas of liturgical reform spread. Beuron is a Benedictine Abbey in the Diocese of Freiburg in south-west Germany. Originally a medieval foundation, but suppressed in 1802, it was restored in 1863 as a Benedictine house by the brothers Maurus and Placidus Wolter, who had learned their Benedictinism at Solesmes.

Maurus was born in 1825 at Bonn and ordained in 1850. In 1857 he was professed as a Benedictine monk in Rome. He and Placidus then returned to Germany and refounded Beuron, Maurus becoming the first abbot. (The similarities with Guéranger's situation are very striking.) The Wolters were strongly influenced by Guéranger and encouraged the promotion of liturgy, Gregorian chant and art, together with some social work. Gradually a Beuronese Congregation developed (formally recognized as such in 1884), with

[5] *Institutions Liturgiques*, Paris, 1878, 92nd edn. III, 210. Quoted in Koenker, p. 144.

[6] Shepherd, op. cit., p. 24.

monasteries in Maredsous (Belgium) – which itself gave rise to Mont César – Erdington (England) and Maria Laach (Germany). Of these, the last was to become particularly influential in the spread of the Liturgical Movement.

The original monastery of Maria Laach (*Maria ad lacum*) in the Rhineland near Coblenz had been founded in 1093. After a varied history the buildings came into the possession of the Beuron Congregation in 1892. Koenker was inclined to see it (despite the earlier work of Beauduin) as the birthplace of the Liturgical Movement: 'The Liturgical Movement as we know it today may . . . be traced to the first of the Liturgical Weeks held for laymen at Maria Laach in Holy Week of 1914.'[7] Something of this influence will be traced in the following chapter.

Selected Reading

B. Capelle, 'Dom Guéranger et l'Esprit Liturgique', in *Questions Liturgiques et Paroissiales*, 12, 1937, pp. 113–46.

H. Ellsworth Chandlee, 'The Liturgical Movement' in J. G. Davies (ed.), *A New Dictionary of Liturgy and Worship*, London, SCM Press, 2nd edn., 1986.

Cuthbert Johnson OSB, *Prosper Guéranger (1805–1875): A Liturgical Theologian*, Studia Anselmiana, Analecta liturgica 9, Rome, 1983.

E. B. Koenker, *The Liturgical Renaissance in the Roman Catholic Church*, Chicago, University of Chicago Press, 1954.

O. Rousseau, *Histoire du Mouvement Liturgique*, 1945.

M. H. Shepherd, *The Liturgical Renewal of the Church*, New York, OUP, 1960.

[7] Koenker, op. cit., p. 12.

4

Rediscovery, Research and Renewal: The Roman Catholic Liturgical Movement 1900–62

Dom Lambert Beauduin of Mont César

In his book *Le Mouvement Liturgique* (ET, *From Silence to Participation*, 1988) Dom Bernard Botte had no hesitation in identifying the beginning of the Liturgical Movement with a paper read at the 1909 Malines Conference by Dom Lambert Beauduin, a Benedictine monk of the Abbey of Mont César, Louvain, in Belgium. As we have seen, there were 'forerunners', and Beauduin himself acknowledged his debt to two people: Dom Prosper Guéranger and Pius X.

The contribution of Guéranger has already been outlined; but what of Pius X? Formerly Giuseppe Sarto, he became Pope in 1903. Before being Bishop of Mantua and Patriarch of Venice, he had had twelve years experience as a parish priest in the parish of Salzano, where he had sought to raise his people's participation in the church's worship, sacraments and festivals.

Three months after his election, on 22 November 1903, he issued a *motu proprio* on church music, which had in many ways got out of hand. From the eighteenth century the increasingly elaborate settings of the Gloria, Creed, etc. were resulting in their being broken up into a series of separate musical items. There were also a tendency for the *Sanctus* to take so long that it was often not completed by the time the celebrant reached the institution narrative. As a result the *Benedictus qui venit* was frequently postponed until after the narrative, destroying the flow and rationale of the canon.

All such aberrations were forbidden in Pius X's *motu proprio*, which Koenker calls 'the fundamental musical directive of the Liturgical Movement'.[1] Instead, the Pope urged the restoration of Gregorian chant 'which recent studies have so happily restored to its original integrity' (a tribute to Guéranger and Solesmes). Indeed, Pius X appointed a committee to revise the Church's song books in which the monks of Solesmes played a major role. However, the Pope's concerns were wider than the mere restoration of Gregorian chant. His encyclical included the sentence:

> In order to restore the true Christian spirit the faithful must be brought back to the first and indispensable source of that spirit, the active participation of the faithful in the holy mysteries and in the public and solemn prayer of the Church.

In 1905 Pius X issued a decree in support of frequent communion, and acquired the nickname of 'the Pope of frequent communion'. This was followed in 1911 by the Bull *Divino afflatu* which reformed the Calendar and Breviary. One of its main features was a redistribution of the Psalter which had been disrupted by the intrusion of saints' days and festivals. Nevertheless, in spite of the work of Pius X, the originality of the approach and ideas found in Beauduin should not be underestimated.

Beauduin was born in 1873, and he entered the monastery of Mont César in 1905 after some years working as what might now be termed an industrial chaplain. In 1907 he was appointed by the Prior to teach dogmatic theology.

It was the Malines Conference of 1909 which provided Beauduin with the opportunity of launching and bringing to public attention the idea of liturgical renewal. His paper was entitled 'The True Prayer of the Church'. His argument proceeded in three stages. He first developed a lesson in fundamental liturgy; then, in contrast, he outlined popular

[1] Koenker, *Liturgical Renaissance*, p. 154.

Christian piety which was quite divorced from the public liturgy; he finally proposed methods for a renewal, arguing that active participation in the liturgy, which is the true source of piety, can be achieved by understanding the liturgical texts. His experience as an industrial priest had led him to the conclusion that Christian society was no longer a fellowship, but divided and individualistic. Piety was no longer based on corporate liturgy, but had become a private matter. The answer was renewal of the liturgical life. He proposed two practical lines of action: a translation of the Latin Missal was to be put in the hands of the Catholic laity; and use of the Daily Office should be encouraged. His views were set out more fully in 1914 in *La Piété de l'Eglise*. Here was revealed the great strength of Beauduin's approach; his Liturgical Movement was underpinned by a theology of the Church as the Mystical Body of Christ, and a theology of priesthood of the laity with a right to active participation in the liturgy.

Beauduin himself began two publications. *La Vie Liturgique* was a monthly publication which gave a translation of the text of the Mass for the coming month, together with popular, pastoral articles on the liturgy. In 1910 there appeared *Questions Liturgiques* (later to become *Questions Liturgiques et Paroissiales*) which was aimed at the clergy, and contained more technical studies. There were also periodic meetings for specialist study, the 'Semaines Liturgiques' which were held at Mont César and elsewhere from 1910, as well as popular 'Liturgical Retreats'. His plan for a liturgical institute did not materialize. All this activity was aimed at the renewal of liturgy at parochial level. Beauduin deserves his claim to the title 'Father of the Liturgical Movement'.

Maria Laach and Klosterneuberg

Whereas Botte (himself a Benedictine from Belgium, and some writers have regarded his claims to be rather nationalistic) saw Beauduin as its real founder, Ernest Koenker claimed that the origins of the Liturgical Movement were to be traced to Germany and Austria, centring on the monasteries of Maria Laach and Klosterneuberg.

According to Koenker, the Liturgical Movement stemmed from a Holy Week conference in 1914 arranged by Abbot Ildephonse Herwegen, and the use of the German Dialogue Mass where the congregation joined with the server in response to the priest. Herwegen was Abbot of Maria Laach from 1913–46, and during his years a number of scholarly publications were begun at Maria Laach which gradually contributed to changing the understanding of the liturgy among clergy and educated laity:

Easter 1918 – *Ecclesia Orans* Series.[2]

1918 – *Liturgiegeschtliche Quellen und Forschungen* which were editions of ancient liturgical texts and scientific monographs edited by Benedictine monks of Maria Laach, Beuron, Emmaus, Coelfeld and Seckau.

1921–41 – *Jahrbuch für Liturgiewissenschaft* (resumed in 1950 as *Archive für Liturgiewissenschaft*) which contained articles and annotated bibliographies of publications on liturgy. Since these were aimed at the clergy and educated laity, they touched a rather limited number of people, and the liturgical movement of Maria Laach was for some time regarded as élitist.

In 1928 Herwegen himself published two pamphlets on the basic tenets of the Liturgical Movement: *Kirche und Seele* and *Christliche Kunst und Mysterium.* In these works he argued that Christianity is not essentially a doctrine, but a life, the life of Christ in the baptized Christian. When the Church celebrates the Divine Mysteries, it participates in the saving work of Christ. He was critical of the subjective individualistic piety which he traced to the Middle Ages,

[2] The first volume by Romano Guardini, *Vom Geist des Liturgie,* ET *The Spirit of the Liturgy,* London, Sheed & Ward, 1930.

challenging the prevailing idea that the Middle Ages was an ideal age. In 1931 Herwegen founded the Institute of Liturgical and Monastic Studies.

Another famous liturgist of Maria Laach was Odo Casel (1886–1948). Shepherd assesses his articles as providing 'the most important single body of theological interpretation of the liturgy in modern times, and their influence has been felt far and wide',[3] though others have been far more critical of his work. His main works were *Die Liturgie als Mysterienfeier* and *Das Christliche Kultmysterium* (summarized in *The Mystery of Christian Worship*, ET 1962) in which he argues that the eucharist is the re-enactment of the mysteries of Christ by the Church (*Mysterienlehre*). For Casel '*Mysterium*' is not intellectual incomprehension, but has three aspects:

1. God in himself – holy and unapproachable.
2. The personal mystery – the incarnation, death, resurrection and ascension are all mysteries 'because God reveals in them in a measure surpassing all human potentialities'.
3. The cult – in which the person and work of Christ are communicated to us:

> The Mysterium is a holy, cultic action in which the redemptive act is rendered present in the rite; since the cultic community accomplishes the rite, it participates in the saving act and through it attains redemption.[4]

In other words, Christ's life and work are made present, operative and effective as the faithful participate in the corporate liturgy.

Casel's work has been criticized on two main grounds. First, he believed that the Christian rites had borrowed from the pagan mystery religions, which more modern scholarship

[3] Shepherd, *Liturgical Renewal*, p. 32.
[4] Odo Casel, *Das Christliche Kultmysterium*, p. 101.

has shown to be quite wrong. Second, his idea of mystery tended to minimize the events of the gospel as once-and-for-all historical events, though Casel himself always rejected this charge.

In Austria the pioneering work was being promulgated by Pius Parsch at the Abbey of Klosterneuberg. Parsch's contribution was to emphasize the importance of the Bible readings in worship, and to show the link between the liturgy and God's record of salvation. Parsch was to found both the 'Volksliturgisches Apostolat' and the periodical *Lebe mit der Kirche* (later *Bibel und Liturgie*).

Behind the ideas of Beauduin, Herwegen and Parsch was, therefore, the pastoral problem of a Latin liturgy recited by a priest with the congregation as spectators. The early leaders of the Liturgical Movement were concerned with the laity as the Body of Christ having a function in the liturgy which should lead to spiritual and social renewal. It was a pastoral movement of renewal through liturgical worship. To achieve its ends the following things were suggested or encouraged:

1. The use of vernacular missals – the Latin in one column, the vernacular in another, so that people could understand what was going on.

2. The use of Gregorian chant with lay people joining in.

3. The use of the Dialogue Mass – the people responding with the server throughout the Mass rather than being preoccupied with their own private devotions.

4. In Germany in particular, in addition to the Latin High Mass and the Dialogue Mass, two other celebrations were encouraged: Mass with German hymns; and German High Mass where most of the service was in German as far as the people were concerned (the priest said the texts in Latin).

5. An emphasis was placed on the Scripture readings, sermons and receiving communion.

The spread of the movement

Despite obvious interruptions caused by the First World War and then the Second World War, the Liturgical Movement began to spread and develop. In France its later leading exponents were Dom Bernard Botte, Père A-M. Roguet OP, Abbé A-G. Martimort, and Louis Bouyer amongst others (see Botte, *From Silence to Participation*). In 1943 the Centre de Pastorale Liturgique was founded, which combined pastoral liturgy with solid research. Its concern was to make liturgy the centre of mission in a secular nation. Its journal was – and continues to be – *La Maison-Dieu*. One of the by-products of the Second World War was that during the German occupation, communication between the French/Belgian and German/Austrian movements was eased, and views were exchanged, resulting in some cross-fertilization.

In the United States of America it was St John's Abbey, Collegeville, which took the lead in liturgical renewal with the publication of the journal *Orate Fratres*, later to become *Worship*. Leading figures in the 1940s and 1950s included Godfrey Diekmann, Gerald Ellard and Frederick McManus (see Chapter 18).

In Germany the movement was pioneered by the Oratorians at Leipzig, who sought to adapt the liturgy to parish conditions. The changes proved attractive, especially to young people who responded to the new solemnity and vitality. In Holland there was also enthusiasm, and the First International Liturgical Week was held at Maastricht in 1946.

In Great Britain things were much slower. As a minority Church, English Catholicism tended to stick close to things Roman and conservative. In 1929 Dom Bernard McElligott of Ampleforth founded the Society of St Gregory 'to maintain the dignity of the sacred liturgy as the supreme instrument of congregational worship'. During the 1930s, Summer Schools were held at Oxford. These were on the pastoral and musical themes of the liturgy. A journal appeared entitled *Music and Liturgy*, subsequently to become *Liturgy*, and finally, *Life and Worship*. Names such as Dom Edmund Jones, Fr J. D. Crichton and Fr Clifford Howell SJ were associated with the English movement.[5] Generally speaking, the English hierarchy were suspicious of the movement, but even so three dioceses gave permission for the Dialogue Mass. Only after the Second World War did the freeze on liturgical renewal begin to thaw – mainly because chaplains serving the forces in Europe had followed their continental brethren.

Research

The Liturgical Movement began, as we have seen, primarily as a pastoral movement of renewal and rediscovery. At a pastoral level it soon became clear that the various Latin rites, particularly the Mass which was the focal point of the movement, were not the greatest of assets in the move for renewal. Latin was a barrier. Furthermore, many parts of the Mass did not seem to have much rationale: there were duplications, too many private prayers for the priest, and the general mode of celebration did not make participation easy. It is not surprising therefore that hand in hand with the pastoral renewal there went a steady scholarly research into liturgy in general. There had, of course, always been distinguished liturgists;[6] in England, for example, there was Edmund Bishop and R. H. Connolly. However, their approach was mainly historical, and they deliberately stopped short of questioning current Roman Catholic dogmatics and practices. A new type of scholarship began to emerge; it was scholarship that questioned the current practices.

We have already noted that Beauduin had started *Questions Liturgique* which was aimed at a more academic

[5] See J. D. Crichton, et al., *English Catholic Worship*.

[6] Louis Bouyer, *Life and Liturgy*.

understanding of liturgical interest. Working with Beauduin was Dom Bernard Capelle of the Abbey Maredsous. He was director of the *Revue Bénédictine,* and later *Recherches de théologie ancienne et mediévale.* His collected papers in *Travaux Liturgiques* show a combination of pastoral and academic papers. Some of these studies were connected with the canon of the Mass, and these studies began to raise some questions about the sense of some parts of this ancient eucharistic prayer. In Belgium the *Dictionnaire d'Archéologie chrétienne et de liturgie* was begun by Dom Fernand Cabrol and Dom Henri Leclercq. In France it was the name of the Belgian scholar Bernard Botte which dominated liturgical scholarship, and it was Botte who brought the attention of Roman Catholic scholars to the importance of the *Apostolic Tradition* of Hippolytus. Botte was later to become the first director of the Institut Supérieur de Liturgie in Paris. Founded in 1956, this was to prepare teachers to teach liturgy in seminaries, and to further liturgical research.

In Germany and Austria Theodor Klauser's *Abendlandische Liturgiegeschichte* 1944 (ET *The Western Liturgy and Its History,* Oxford 1952) and Joseph Jungmann's *Missarum Solemnia* 1949 (ET *The Mass of the Roman Rite,* New York 1951–52) provided studies of the origin of the Roman rite, with implications for reform. C. Mohlberg produced a series of new editions of the older sacramentaries, and Andrieu published the *Ordines Romani.* The publications associated with Herwegen and Odo Casel have already been mentioned. Important also was the founding of the Liturgical Institute at Trier in 1947 under the Directorship of Dr Johannes Wagner. Conferences were organized to explain the new understanding of worship and to further both pastoral and academic studies.

One result of this research was that what had hitherto been a movement urging renewal was beginning to be a movement which hinted at the desirability of some reform.

Mediator Dei 1947

It was fairly clear that the spread of the Liturgical Movement would never achieve its ultimate goals throughout the Catholic Church without some positive official encouragement from Rome. A *motu proprio* of 1903 was hardly enough. The official endorsement and encouragement was forthcoming in the encyclical of 1947 called *Mediator Dei*. It has been described as the 'Magna Carta' of the Liturgical Movement. J-D. Benoit wrote: 'This, like most encyclicals, does not inaugurate a new movement in the Church; rather does it bear witness to the reality and vitality of a movement already in existence.'[7]

By many inside the Liturgical Movement, *Mediator Dei* was seen as an attack on, and condemnation of, what they were trying to achieve. Certain practices which it sees as aberrations are condemned (e.g. altars in the form of tables, Christus Rex figures on crucifixes instead of the suffering Christ, suppression of popular spiritual exercises), but a more detached assessment reveals a more positive aspect: '. . . any fair-minded reading of this document makes evident the Pope's sincere support of the basic aims and many of the methods of Liturgical Movement leaders'.[8]

In its introduction *Mediator Dei* gave official recognition to the Liturgical Movement, and it singled out for special mention the Benedictines. Part of the encyclical repudiated the suggestion that there is opposition between subjective and objective worship, and this, together with some other statements of warning, was interpreted by some as a repudiation of some of the ideas which emanated from Maria Laach as set out by Herwegen and Odo Casel. The encyclical made three important points:

1. In the liturgy there were both human and divine elements; the human elements may be modified.

[7] Benoit, *Liturgical Renewal*, p. 70. Benoit goes on to liken *Mediator Dei* to secateurs, cutting out suckers so as to encourage healthy growth (p. 72).

[8] Shepherd, op. cit., p. 36.

2. Although modifications are due to the needs of the faithful, the ultimate determination of the changes rests with the ecclesiastical authority.

3. Changes in the liturgy are a positive good and are evidence of the Church's vitality.

However, the encyclical warned against liturgical archaeologism – the re-creation of the past because the past was supposed to be better. Nevertheless, it did explain the role of the faithful in the liturgy. By reason of their baptism, Christians are in the Mystical Body, and therefore join in the liturgy. Participation is achieved by reciting prayers, offering with and through the priest, and by self-offering. Furthermore, the use of the vernacular could be an advantage to the people in certain rites (which led to the use of the vernacular in certain German and French Rituals). However it also stressed that since not everyone can read, 'private' religious devotion is a valid way of participating. Although encouraging regular communion, the document reiterated that only the priest needs to communicate.

From *Mediator Dei* to Vatican II

Mediator Dei represented an important watershed in the Liturgical Movement. Up until this point the movement had been concerned with renewal; now change was hinted at. During the next few years a number of small but significant changes came from Rome:

1951 (9 Feb.) The Easter Vigil was experimentally restored on an optional basis.

1953 (6 Jan.) The Apostolic Constitution *Christus Dominus* allowed evening Masses under certain conditions, and relaxed the rules of fasting.

1955 (23 Mar.) A General Decree simplified the calendar, and the rubrics of the Mass and Divine Office.

1955 (16 Nov.) The restoration of the entire Holy Week ceremonies, which were to be celebrated on the correct days at the appropriate times.[9]

These official changes, together with the lukewarm encouragement of Liturgical Congresses, gave rise to an expectation of greater change, and more activity in terms of renewal and study resulted. In 1953 the movement made its mark in Ireland with an annual conference arranged at Glenstal Abbey, some of the papers appearing under the title *Studies in Pastoral Liturgy*. In England an annual conference of pastoral liturgy met at Spode House in Staffordshire from 1962. There was also a demand for services in the vernacular, despite the plea by Christine Morhmann that Latin was a hieratic or sacred language. However, the main pressure came from France and Germany, from the Centre de Pastorale Liturgique and the Liturgical Institute at Trier. These two institutions organized congresses of liturgical experts concerned with plans for revision, in the hope of bringing pressure to bear on Rome. The first of these was held at Maria Laach in 1951, where problems of the Missal and the Lectionary were discussed. At the congress at Assisi, Botte noted that 'officialdom' made its appearance – a cardinal was sent to preside – and a certain restraint was placed on what had hitherto been frank discussion. But the presence of 'officialdom' meant that the Vatican took the congresses seriously. Indeed, in his address to the congresses Pius XII said that the Liturgical Movement was a sign of the passage of the Holy Spirit on the Church. By the mid-1950s the leading European Catholic liturgists had prepared themselves for the event of reform; if and when it came, they had done their homework, and had blueprints at the ready.

[9] For the minutiae, see Gerald Ellard, *The Mass in Transition*.

Selected Reading

Lambert Beauduin, *Liturgy the Life of the Church*, trans. V. Michel, Collegeville, Liturgical Press, 1929.

J-D. Benoit, *Liturgical Renewal. Studies in Catholic and Protestant Developments on the Continent*, Studies in Ministry and Worship 5, London, Lutterworth, 1958.

Bernard Botte, *From Silence to Participation*, ET John Sullivan, Washington, The Pastoral Press, 1988.

Louis Bouyer, *Life and Liturgy*, London, Sheed & Ward, 1956.

Odo Casel, *The Mystery of Christian Worship*, London, DLT, 1962.

J. D. Crichton, H. E. Winstone, J. R. Ainslie, *English Catholic Worship*, London, Geoffrey Chapman, 1979.

Gerald Ellard, *The Mass in Transition*, Milwaukee, Bruce, 1956.

Ernest B. Koenker, *The Liturgical Renaissance in the Roman Catholic Church*, Chicago, University of Chicago Press, 1954.

Priests of St Severin and St Joseph, *What is the Liturgical Movement*, London, Burns & Oates, 1964.

M. H. Shepherd, *The Liturgical Renewal of the Church*, New York, OUP, 1960.

J. H. Srawley, *The Liturgical Movement, its Origin and Growth*, Alcuin Club Tract 27, London, Mowbray, 1954.

5

The Anglican Church and the Liturgical Movement I

Historically the Liturgical Movement was a Roman Catholic movement. The problems which faced Dom Lambert Beauduin and Abbot Herwegen, however, were pastoral problems which were shared by many other European Churches. It is not surprising, therefore, that the insights of this Catholic movement had parallel stirrings in other Churches, and in turn influenced, and then were developed in non-Roman Catholic ways in other Churches. The 1951 Report of the Faith and Order Commission on Worship, under the auspices of the World Council of Churches, stated: 'In the course of this enquiry we have been struck by the extent to which a "liturgical movement" is to be found in churches of widely differing traditions.'[1] In many of the Western Churches we find a similar pattern to that in the Roman Catholic Church – a period of rediscovery, research and renewal, and then, particularly in the 1960s, a deluge of new liturgical rites. In this chapter we are concerned with the Anglican Church, and particularly the Church of England.

Forerunners and false trails

The Reformation ideal

The ideal of the English Reformers was a weekly eucharist with the congregation receiving communion. Baptism was

[1] P. Edwall, E. Hayman and W. D. Maxwell (eds), *Ways of Worship*, London, SCM Press, 1951, p. 16.

to be a community event involving the whole congregation at public worship. The *Book of Common Prayer* also assumed that there would be daily morning and evening prayers in the parish church with a congregation. For all sorts of reasons these ideals – some of which were entirely consonant with those of the Liturgical Movement – were seldom achieved.

Eighteenth-century High Churchmen, and John Wesley

In the eighteenth century a number of High Churchmen, standing in the tradition of Archbishop Laud and Bishop Andrewes, some of whom were later to become Non-jurors (those who could not take the oath of allegiance to William and Mary after 1689), began to devise private liturgies based on their research of the ancient rites, particularly Apostolic Constitutions VIII and St James. Among these were Edward Stephens and Thomas Rattray.[2] Historic liturgies and the centrality of the eucharist were brought to the attention of the Church of England.

John Wesley, influenced by his Oxford University background, his apparent failure in America, and his meeting with members of the Unitas Fratrum (Moravians), began the Methodist revival in the Church of England. The main emphasis of early Methodism was on preaching of the gospel as personal faith rather than on the colder moralism which typified many Anglican sermons of the time, and on regular attendance at Holy Communion. Methodism developed a preaching service, possibly based on the University Sermon and its accompanying bidding prayer, which was to supplement the 1662 diet of worship. As it was developed by Methodist preachers it came to include extempore prayer and hymns.[3] As Wesley became more

[2] W. Jardine Grisbrooke, *Anglican Liturgies of the Seventeenth and Eighteenth Centuries*, Alcuin Club Collection 40, London, SPCK, 1958.

[3] Adrian Burdon, *The Preaching Service – the Glory of the Methodists*, Alcuin/GROW Liturgical Study 17, Bramcote, Grove Books, 1991.

and more estranged from the Established Church, and after he ordained ministers for America, he himself undertook a light abridgement of the Prayer Book in 1784. Wesley was concerned to put preaching and the eucharist at the centre of church life.

The Tractarians and the Camden Society

The Oxford Movement, or Tractarian Movement, traced its own origins to the Assize Sermon delivered on 14 July 1833 by John Keble, and the meeting at Hadleigh Rectory, 15–19 July 1833. Keble, Pusey and Newman, together with H. J. Rose and a few others, launched a campaign to recall the Church of England to its apostolic roots. The first generation Tractarians were concerned with church order, and decency in worship. They were staunch defenders of the Prayer Book, including many of its rubrics which had fallen into disuse. At the heart of their theology was a concern for the centrality of the sacraments. The second generation saw the development of the 'ritualists' who re-introduced ceremonial into the celebration of the eucharist. The Tracts produced by the original founders were concerned to stress ecclesiastical and sacramental principles and doctrine which could be worked out in worship and discipline. At Cambridge the Camden Society was founded in 1839 by J. M. Neale and B. Webb for the study of ecclesiastical architecture and art; it was later renamed the Ecclesiological Society. Through its periodical, *The Ecclesiologist*, it advocated the revival of Gothic architecture for church building, and promoted Catholic forms of worship and ceremonial. Its advocacy of a return to a medieval style of architecture included the concern for a sanctuary and high altar rather than an auditorium-type building. Dignified worship and the centrality of eucharistic worship were at the heart of this movement.[4]

[4] A. Hardelin, *The Tractarian Understanding of the Eucharist*, Uppsala 1965; J. F. White, *The Cambridge Movement*, Cambridge, CUP, 1962, 1979.

Christian Socialism

In his book *Earth and Altar* Donald Gray has argued that in England the true forerunners or originators of the Liturgical Movement were the Christian Socialists. Their ideas can be found in the writings of F. D. Maurice, S. T. Coleridge, J. M. Ludlow and Charles Kingsley, and were developed by priests who combined their ideas with those of the Tractarians. Exponents included Henry Scott Holland, J. R. Illingworth, E. S. Talbot and Charles Gore, and their ideas were expressed in the collection of essays, *Lux Mundi* (1890), and in organizations such as the Guild of St Matthew, The Christian Social Union and The Christian Socialist League. The eucharist was promoted as the continuous expression of the incarnation, being the means of our union with God and one another. The eucharistic fellowship was the cornerstone of fellowship and brotherhood of all humanity. At a pastoral and practical level a direct result was the establishment of the Parish Communion. Gray argues that the Parish Communion movement in England has its origins in Christian Socialism, and was quite independent of the Roman Catholic Liturgical Movement. 'Without any detectable borrowing from comparable Roman Catholic Liturgical Movement which was developing on the Continent of Europe, the idea of the Parish Communion began to take place in the 1920s and 1930s'.[5] He traces the influence of the movement through the late nineteenth century to the twentieth century, in such figures as W. E. Moll, whose curates included Conrad Noel of Thaxted fame.

With regard to the establishment of a Parish Communion which has to come to be regarded as the touchstone of the English Liturgical Movement, there are many claimants to be the first. Thus, for example, an 8.00 a.m. Sung Eucharist is recorded at Frome in 1852; a 9.00 a.m. Merbecke Eucharist was established at Middlesborough in 1893. In 1905 Cosmo Lang in *The Opportunity of the Church of England* advocated

[5] Gray, *Earth and Altar*, p. xii.

a 9 or 9.30 a.m. Parish Communion, and this was perhaps the first use of the term in print.

W. H. Frere: Some Principles of Liturgical Reform

One result of the concern of the second generation Tractarians with ceremonial and vestments was a series of lawsuits brought by Evangelicals in an attempt to declare ritualistic practices illegal. Eventually a Royal Commission was appointed, which reported in 1906, concluding that 'the law of public worship in the Church of England is too narrow for the religious life of the present generation'. The Report recommended that Letters of Business be issued to the Convocations with instructions to frame new rubrics and a new liturgy. The process was to drag on until 1928. However, one prominent person involved in the process was W. H. Frere, who in 1911 published *Some Principles of Liturgical Reform*. He advocated a modest revision of the Prayer Book with the removal of archaisms and obsolete rubrics. In this book he argued for 'a celebration of Holy Communion at which it is suitable for the people to communicate, and this must form the chief service of the day'.[6]

Chaplains of the First World War

The experience of the chaplains serving in the First World War was gathered together in the hope that the Church of England might learn something from this ministry to men, many of whom had never had any church connection, or who had ceased to have any connection. The chaplains discovered that many men in the trenches were deeply religious in the sense of having deep views about right and wrong, love and hate, and basic Christian views and ideals. However, they saw no connection between these and the Established Church and its worship. The report on worship, *The Worship of the Church*, made a number of observations

[6] Frere, *Some Principles of Liturgical Reform*, London, John Murray, 1911, p. 154.

and recommendations, one of which was to argue that the parish eucharist should be the centre of Anglican worship, and that liturgical revision should be linked with a programme of education and pastoral action. Sadly, most of these recommendations were ignored, and the Church of England continued to fail to provide a liturgy which appealed to the 'working class'.[7]

The 1927/8 Prayer Book

The process of revision initiated by the Royal Commission dragged on through the First World War and beyond, with the different ecclesiastical parties all attempting to steer the course of the revision. The resulting book failed to get parliamentary approval on two occasions. Perhaps it was as well. The type of revision represented in this tragic book suggests the following concerns: the preservation of as much of 1662 as possible; the liturgical fancies of Bishop W. F. Frere, and of moderate Anglo-Catholics. Most of the energies of this revision went into ideas of consecration with an epiclesis, and reservation of the Blessed Sacrament, which might rightly be regarded as the dregs of liturgical activity. However, revision in the Church of England did spark off and encourage revision in other parts of the Anglican Communion, without parliamentary interference. A number of interesting Anglican liturgies date from around 1928. Of some interest also was the Liturgy of Bombay, 1922, which attempted to combine Syrian liturgical sources (in use in India for many centuries) with Prayer Book material. This was an early attempt at 'inculturation', even if its use was never very great.

Just as the Roman Catholic Liturgical Movement initiated by Beauduin and Herwegen can be seen to be a result of earlier influences, so also the pioneers of the Liturgical Movement in England were consciously and unconsciously drawing on the fruits and inspiration of forerunners, even

[7] Ibid., pp. 35–50.

if some of these, such as the official revision of the 1927/8 Prayer Book, were something of a false trail.

Henry de Candole and A. G. Hebert

It was in the 1930s that the insights of the continental Liturgical Movement developed by Beauduin and Herwegen began to be mediated directly to the Anglican Church. At a pastoral level the pioneer active from about 1934, and still alive to be able to take part in Church of England and Joint Liturgical Group revision, was Henry de Candole (1895–1971), later Bishop of Knaresborough.

De Candole came from an Evangelical background, but as a teenager occasionally attended All Saints Clifton where he learned to love the beauty, ceremony, and centrality of the eucharist. After graduating from Cambridge he trained at Westcott House, and for a time was a schoolmaster at Marlborough College. Between 1923–26 he was domestic chaplain to Archbishop Davidson, and in 1925 represented the Archbishop at an Orthodox wedding which deeply impressed him. He also watched the bishops meeting to work on the ill-fated Prayer Book for 1927: 'I came to realize how entirely ignorant they were about liturgy, except for a bare fraction – Frere was almost alone.'[8] De Candole became a reader of *Questions Liturgique*, and as a curate at St John's, Newcastle (1926–31) was involved in developing the Parish Communion there. For health reasons he had to give up this work, and from 1932–34 he was Chaplain of Peterhouse, Cambridge. It was there that he wrote two short books, *The Church's Offering: A brief study of Eucharistic Worship*, and *The Sacraments and the Church: A Study in the corporate nature of Christianity*, both published in 1935. In a pamphlet entitled 'The Parish Communion', 1936, he outlined the reason why the Parish Communion rather than Matins or a non-

[8] Quoted by Jagger, *Henry de Candole*, p. 55.

communicating High Mass should be the main service on a Sunday:

1. The eucharist is a corporate offering.
2. We come to give.
3. Communion is an essential part of this worship.
4. The 'Family' eucharist is the centre of the 'family' life.

The centrality of the eucharist, communicating attendance, and the corporate nature of the Church were his main teaching themes when Chaplain at Chichester Theological College, 1935–37. He then became Liturgical Missioner for the Chichester diocese; this was an honorary appointment without stipend. However, it gave him the opportunity to speak within the diocese and elsewhere on the Liturgical Movement and the Parish Communion. In 1939 he could explain his views as follows:

> Christian Worship is the Christian community offering its life and work to God through our Lord. Liturgy means the activity of the people of God, which is primarily a corporate common activity of the whole fellowship. That action is one of offering, and most clearly set forth and illustrated in the Eucharist, which is the heart of Christian worship.[9]

He also admitted: 'My regret, all this time, was that we "Liturgical Movement people" were so little in touch with Evangelicals.'[10]

Similar ideas were presented by Fr A. G. Hebert (1886–1963) in his book *Liturgy and Society* (1935).[11] Hebert was born in 1886 at Silloth Vicarage in Cumberland. He studied at New College, Oxford, and trained at Cuddesdon. He later joined the Society of the Sacred Mission, the Kelham Fathers. In articles in the *SSM Quarterly* he advocated the eucharist – Parish Communion – being the centre of Anglican worship, and explained some of the principles of the Roman

[9] Ibid., p. 119.
[10] Ibid., p. 122.
[11] See Irvine, *Worship, Church and Society*.

Catholic Liturgical Movement. In *Liturgy and Society* Hebert condemned the individualism of the age, and stressed that Christianity is about community and a collective. Regular church people are moulded by the liturgy. In baptism a person is consecrated, and receives a share in Divinity. Citing Herwegen, Hebert taught that Christianity is a mystery, where the past is made present. The liturgy is a corporate offering of the whole people of God. The corporate nature of the Church was a key to a more corporate mankind. Here we can see the similarity to the Christian Socialists. Nevertheless, in this book the quintessence of the Roman Catholic Liturgical Movement was made available to the Anglican Church.

In 1935 Brother Edward wrote to Hebert exhorting him to publish a collection of essays on the subject of the Liturgical Movement and the Parish Communion. Brother Edward – Edward Gordon Bulstrode – had for a short time been with the Cowley Fathers (Society of St John the Evangelist) at Oxford, but settled at Temple Balsall from where he conducted an itinerate apostolate. He was a great advocate of the Parish Communion. Hebert was persuaded, and the result was a symposium entitled *The Parish Communion* (1937). Gray comments: 'The book was produced just two years after the publication of *Liturgy and Society*, and 2,500 copies were sold in the first nine months, proof positive, if it was needed of an unfulfilled appetite.'[12]

The symposium was edited by Hebert, and de Candole was one of the contributors. In these essays it was emphasized that instead of an 8 a.m. communion, with an 11 a.m. non-communicating High Mass or Matins, the ideal should be the 9.30 a.m. Parish Communion, followed by a Parish Breakfast. People would communicate, and not simply be present. The bread and wine of the eucharist represent the whole substance of our lives, all our joys, sorrows, plans for the future, our hopes and fears. Here we see the beginning

[12] Gray, op. cit., p. 206.

of an emphasis on the offertory procession which became part of this pastoral movement.

In Essay IV Austin Farrar, the celebrated Oxford Anglo-Catholic theologian, was to argue that the Church is Christ's Mystical Body, and it is the overflow of his Glorious Body: 'for in so far as we are members of the Body, we are nothing but Christ. It is not we that live, but He that lives in us, and is the substance of our redeemed existence'.[13]

This led the way for Gregory Dix in Essay V to state that the incarnation was extended in the Church and the eucharist. The 1552/1662 communion service was mentioned as failing to express the corporate nature of the Church. Four actions – mentioned by Hebert in his 1935 book – were now expounded briefly by Dix – takings, thanking, breaking and giving. The offertory procession – the solemn presentation of the bread and wine, usually by members of the congregation – was justified on the grounds that it expressed the common priesthood of the Church. The book also emphasizes psalmody at the eucharist, and the '10 minute liturgical sermon'.

Brother Edward himself was to edit a small collection in 1938, *Sunday Morning: The New Way. Papers on the Parish Communion.*

Parish and People

As on the Continent, the progress of the Liturgical Movement in the Church of England was interrupted by the Second World War. But in 1947, a meeting between Henry de Candole, Kenneth Packard (who was also attracted to the ideals of *Questions Liturgiques*, having visited France and seen something of the Liturgical Movement there), and Patrick McLaughlin (Vicar of St Anne's, Soho) gradually led to the founding in 1949 of Parish and People. This was very much the embodiment of the Liturgical Movement on

[13] Hebert (ed.), *Parish Communion*, p. 80.

English soil. Its pioneers believed that it was inspired by the Holy Spirit. Its opening manifesto stated:

> We are not, therefore, concerned with the details of rites and ceremonies and form of words, not merely with the history of their origins and development, not merely with popularising the Book of Common Prayer . . . our approach to liturgy is not that of the SPCK omnibus volume *Liturgy and Worship* but rather that of Fr Hebert's great and prophetic book *Liturgy and Society*. Liturgy is to the Church what the four-square walls of new Jerusalem are to the City of God – the framework of order which defines and shapes the common life of the Beloved Community, of parish and people.[14]

The journal of the movement was simply called *Parish and People*. Since liturgy is not just confined to services, but infects the life of the Church, the interests of the movement spread from establishing the Parish Communion to complete renewal of parish life. A later pamphlet, *Parish and People. What is it?* (1960), stated:

> The object of the Parish and People Movement is to help members of the Church of England and its sister Churches in and beyond the Anglican Communion to understand better:
>
> (a) THE BIBLE, in particular what it makes known about God and His people, the Church.
>
> (b) WORSHIP, especially as it is corporately offered by the People of God in Holy Communion.
>
> (c) CHRISTIAN ACTION, as the people of God are sent to live in the world in order to transform the world.

Parish and People arranged conferences and liturgical missions to the parishes.

One influential member of Parish and People was Ernest Southcott, who began a House Church system on the Halton Moor Estate in Leeds. Malcolm Boyd wrote:

> The kitchen table is set up within the living room in one of the compact slum-clearance dwellings. Used candles from the altar at the parish church are placed upon the table that becomes the

[14] *Parish and People. What is it all about?*, p. 4.

> altar . . . Home-made bread, the same bread that the family had eaten for tea the night before is used for the service. The Bible and last evening's newspaper are close together; and they will shortly be in the same conversation, too.[15]

In 1963 Parish and People merged with the Keble Conference Group, and from this point its concerns became much wider than simply liturgy; the influence of the Keble Conference meant that it too became concerned with a new reformation programme. Renewal within the structure of the Church of England in turn was replaced with an ecumenical concern, and in 1970 Parish and People was wound up, and merged with the ecumenical group called ONE. For some twenty years, however, Parish and People was a spearhead of the Liturgical Movement in England. De Candole was to claim: '"our" efforts . . . have borne wonderful fruit to the changing of the face of Sunday Worship throughout the country'.[16] Michael Marshall wrote:

> It is perhaps the 'parish and people movement' which has done more than any other single movement to unchurch the people of the United Kingdom. It insisted on one sort of service (exclusively the Eucharist) for one sort of people at one sort of time. We must now recover a healthy diversity which is truly catholic in its flexibility.[17]

Liturgical scholarship and a Liturgical Commission

Another important side to the Roman Catholic Liturgical Movement was research into the history and theology of worship. This also had an Anglican counterpart. Hebert himself was no mean scholar, but it was the name of Gregory Dix which dominated liturgical study from the 1940s.

[15] Malcolm Boyd, *Crisis in Communication: A Christian Examination of the Mass Media*, New York, p. 83.

[16] Jagger, *Henry de Candole*, p. 131.

[17] Michael Marshall, *Renewal in Worship*, Marshall, Morgan & Scott, London, 1982, p. 62.

Dom Gregory Dix (George Eglinton Alston 1901–52) was a historian by training, and was ordained in 1924. Later he entered Nashdom Abbey, an Anglican Benedictine community, and was eventually to become Prior. Already in 1934 he had written on the epiclesis, and in 1937 published a critical edition of *The Apostolic Tradition*. In 1938 a paper appeared in *Theology* which showed a very different line of approach to the eucharistic prayer to that of W. H. Frere. Although Dix was also to write an important work on confirmation, it is his massive tome *The Shape of the Liturgy* (1945) which has given him a lasting place in the history of English liturgy. The book had a large impact for a number of reasons. First – which was quite remarkable for a liturgical textbook – it was readable and witty. Again, it was comprehensive, covering a vast span of liturgical history. In one book the liturgical findings which were scattered in obscure journals were brought together and presented in a lucid manner. And third, Dix was not simply an historian; he used the material to hint at ideas for future projects of revision.

The central message of *The Shape* was the theory of the four-action shape. As we have noted, Hebert had already mentioned four actions of the eucharist in *Liturgy and Society*, but without any elaboration. In his essay in *The Parish Communion*, Dix expounded the four actions with reference to Hippolytus's *The Apostolic Tradition*. Now in *The Shape*, the theory was given extended treatment. In the New Testament accounts of the eucharist Dix claimed that there is a 'seven-action scheme', which the ancient liturgies reproduce as four:

> With absolute unanimity the liturgical tradition reproduces these seven actions as four: (1) The offertory; bread and wine are 'taken' and placed on the table together. (2) The prayer; the president gives thanks to God over bread and wine together. (3) The fraction; the bread is broken. (4) The communion; the bread and wine are distributed together.

> In that form and in that order these four actions constituted the absolutely invariable nucleus of every eucharist rite known to us throughout antiquity from the Euphrates to Gaul.

Dix noted that this shape was not expressed clearly in the Prayer Book rite.

Dix's arguments and evidence are flawed,[18] but the theory was accepted by many Anglicans, and the four-action pattern has been the foundation of a host of modern Anglican rites.[19]

A great popularizer of Dixian and Parish and People ideas was J. A. T. Robinson, Suffragan Bishop of Woolwich, whose collection of short essays *Liturgy Coming to Life* (1960) helped establish their ideas at parish level.

Two other important scholars who dominated liturgical study from the late 1940s through to the early 1960s were Edward Craddock Ratcliff and Arthur Hubert Couratin. Ratcliff (1896–1967) was successively lecturer in liturgy at Oxford, Professor at King's College, London, and then Ely Professor and Regius Professor at Cambridge. Couratin (1902–88) became Principal of St Stephen's House, Oxford, and took over the teaching of liturgy in the University; in his latter years he was Canon Librarian at Durham, and taught liturgy for Durham University. Both of these scholars were mainly concerned with the early Roman traditions, though Ratcliff was an orientalist who also wrote on early Syrian liturgy. Ratcliff put forward the theory that the eucharistic prayer of *The Apostolic Tradition* had originally concluded with the Sanctus – a view which Couratin supported. When these scholars did write on the Anglican Prayer Book, it was with appreciation for Cranmer's method, though they themselves did not find the Prayer Book congenial to their convictions, theological or liturgical.

[18] Bryan D. Spinks, 'Mis-Shapen: Gregory Dix and the Four-Action Shape of the Liturgy', *The Lutheran Quarterly*, 4 (1990), pp. 161–77.

[19] K. W. Stevenson, *Gregory Dix 25 Years On*, Grove Liturgical Study 10, Bramcote, Grove Books, 1977.

Mention should also be made of Geoffrey G. Willis (1914–82), who wrote on the Roman rite, and Bernard Wigan (1918–94) who collected together and published the main eucharistic rites of the Anglican Communion.

In October 1954 both Convocations of the Church of England passed a resolution asking that the Archbishops should jointly appoint a Standing Liturgical Commission. The Commission first met with Colin Dunlop, then Dean of Lincoln, as its chairman. Ronald Jasper has commented:

> ... it was a fairly academic group with considerable expertise in liturgy and doctrine laced with parochial experience, and with a broad representation of churchmanship. It was limited, however, in having no diocesan bishops or lay persons among its members; but in the climate of the mid-fifties this was probably not surprising, for its work was regarded as that of a rather specialist group.[20]

The Commission produced two reports which were to affect liturgical revision in the Anglican Communion – *Prayer Book Revision in the Church of England* (1957) and, less directly, *The Commemoration of Saints and Heroes of the Faith in the Anglican Communion* (1958). These were prepared for the Lambeth Conference 1958, which itself became a landmark in the Liturgical Movement in the Anglican Church.

Selected Reading

Donald Gray, *Earth and Altar*, Norwich, Alcuin Club/Canterbury Press, 1986.

A. G. Hebert, *Liturgy and Society*, London, Faber & Faber, 1935.

— (ed.), *The Parish Communion*, London, SPCK, 1937.

C. Irvine, *Worship, Church and Society*, Norwich, Canterbury Press, 1993.

P. J. Jagger, *Bishop Henry de Candole. His Life and Times*, London, Faith Press, 1974.

[20] R. C. D. Jasper, *The Development of the Anglican Liturgy 1662–1980*, London, SPCK, 1989, p. 211.

P. J. Jagger, *A History of the Parish and People Movement*, London, Faith Press, 1978.

D. M. Paton (ed.), *The Parish Communion Today*, London, SPCK, 1962.

6

South Indian Springboard

'It all began . . . in South India.'[1]

By the middle of the twentieth century much of the groundwork needed for liturgical reform had taken place. Good ancient models had been identified, principles were emerging, and the deficiencies of current forms increasingly recognized. Throughout much of the World Church something like a consensus among liturgists was being reached. The difficulty was that little of this had reached the mainstream life of the major Churches. The Western-rite Roman Catholic Church was still firmly wedded to the Tridentine Mass; the Eastern Churches had no desire to change their ancient liturgies; the Churches of the Anglican Communion looked on the Book of Common Prayer as an unalterable element in their unity; the Lutherans had settled down to various time-honoured patterns; and the Protestant Churches did not consider themselves 'liturgical' in a way that made it easy to absorb the insights of the Liturgical Movement. Moreover, few of the Churches had in place any constitutional 'machinery' by which to undertake liturgical reform.

What was needed was a Church that would be willing to take the risk of re-ordering its worshipping practice in line with the discoveries and aims of the Liturgical Movement, and so to act as model or trail-blazer for other Churches. In

[1] C. O. Buchanan, in *Liturgy Reshaped*, p. 146.

the event the Church that fulfilled that role was the Church of South India.

The Church of South India (CSI) came into existence on 27 September 1947, as a result of the union of some of the dioceses of the Anglican Church of India, Pakistan, Burma and Ceylon, with the South India Province of the Methodist Church, the South India United Church (SICU – itself the result of a Presbyterian/Congregational union in 1908) and the Basel Mission. It was the first-ever union of episcopal and non-episcopal Churches. Moreover, although the uniting Churches owed their particular traditions to the Western European Reformation and subsequent developments, their union and search for common liturgical forms took place in precisely that part of India which was home to the ancient St Thomas Christians whose Eastern rites could be traced back to the earliest centuries of the Church. Thus Anglican, Protestant and Orthodox insights formed the background to the new Church, and all three strands were to contribute to its liturgy.

The search for church unity in India may conveniently be traced back to the Tranquebar Conference of 1919 when members of the SIUC met with Anglican clergy. The conference agreed that episcopacy as a form of church government need not call into question the 'spiritual equality' of all believers, nor did it imply any particular theory of 'apostolic succession'. The conversations which ensued were joined in 1925 by the Methodists and by 1929 a first draft *Scheme of Union* was produced. This was to go through many stages before the seventh and final draft was produced in 1941. The end of the Second World War and the imminent prospect of Indian independence made the need for a united witness by an independent Indian Church even more urgent. In 1946 the four Anglican bishops involved announced that after union they would receive communion from non-episcopally ordained ministers. This resolved a theological impasse and the scheme obtained the necessary approvals. There was no re-ordination of non-episcopally ordained clergy, but all subsequent ordinations were to be episcopal. The resultant 'mixed' ministry attracted much criticism from parts of the Anglican Communion in particular, and led to a degree of isolation. Fortunately this did not extend to the liturgical creations of the CSI.

The initial intention had been that the different traditions in the CSI would continue their own patterns of worship. Soon, however, the need began to be felt for a common form which could be used on diocesan and similar occasions. In 1948 therefore, the first Synod of the CSI appointed a Liturgy Committee with Leslie Brown as its Convenor. Brown was an English Anglican presbyter, of Evangelical persuasion. As an ordinand he had struck up a friendship – rather unusual for one of his position in those days – with Fr Gabriel Hebert of Kelham. He thus became exposed to the thinking of the Liturgical Movement: 'I had been thoroughly indoctrinated by the books of Father Gabriel Hebert, *Liturgy and Society*, and *The Parish Communion*.'[2] Brown's theoretical conviction was reinforced by practice: he served as an assistant curate in an English parish where the Parish Communion was the main Sunday morning service.

Early in 1948 the Executive of the CSI Synod wrote to Brown asking that his committee prepare a new eucharistic liturgy. Brown, who had never seriously contemplated using anything other than the *Book of Common Prayer*, began the task. Owing to the large distances involved and the cost of travel for a poor Church, much of the committee's work was done by correspondence. There seemed to be three possibilities: a revision of the *Book of Common Prayer*; a version of the Liturgy of St James (the main eucharistic liturgy of the St Thomas Christians); or the production of an entirely new liturgy incorporating elements from the traditions of the uniting Churches. The third option was chosen. Brown himself prepared the first draft: 'First I tried to put down every element of worship that was needed for

[2] Brown, *Relevant Liturgy*, p. 17.

a complete Sunday service for the people of God. I then tried to arrange this material into what seemed a logical order, and I deliberately tried to avoid constant changes of posture.'[3]

The Liturgy of the Word was to be capable of standing as a complete service in itself, to be used whenever there was no presbyter present, which was a not uncommon experience in some of the scattered congregations. The influence of liturgical scholarship showed in Brown's choice of the rite of Hippolytus as one of his main models. He had contemplated using material from the Liturgy of John Chrysostom, but in the end decided that the *Book of Common Prayer*'s stress on the uniqueness of Christ's sacrifice was more appropriate for India. The Bible, as obviously common to the uniting traditions, was to be the primary source of imagery and concepts.

Full congregational participation was another basic principle. There was clearly Anglican precedent for joint recitation of prayers and responsorial patterns, but Brown extended this into the eucharistic prayer itself. In this he was drawing on local Orthodox practice: the anaphora of the Liturgy of St James is punctuated by congregational acclamations. Thus, anaphoral acclamations were introduced into the CSI rite and from there were to become extremely widespread in the revised rites of other Churches.

The Peace is another widespread feature which owes its modern usage to Indian origins. Although clearly a basic element in the early Church, in subsequent centuries it had either died out altogether (sometimes without even a verbal trace) or been reduced to a stylized greeting between the clergy. Among the Syrian-rite St Thomas Christians it had, however, continued as a hand-to-hand greeting passed among the congregation. Ancient precedent and modern local practice therefore suggested its inclusion in the new CSI rite. At one stage, however, this was opposed by CSI

[3] Brown, *Three Worlds*, p. 76.

Bishop C. K. Jacob (himself of Syrian stock) who felt that the passing of the Peace was an act of hypocrisy in the Syrian Churches, torn as they were by dissensions and lawsuits. Brown recalls that Bishop Jacob's objection was opposed by others on the committee, especially the Methodists, who had experimented with it and found it 'a moment of glad surprise'.[4] It was thus incorporated into the rite and so found an international acceptance which goes far beyond what the CSI Liturgy Committee could ever have envisaged. Lesslie Newbigin, another prominent member of the Liturgical Committee, was to look back in later years with amazement: 'We did not know in those exciting discussions that what we were doing would give a lead to changes in liturgy all over the world for several decades to come.'[5]

The same is perhaps true of the use of the westward position of the celebrant at the eucharist. In suggesting this position Brown was aware that it had the sanction of primitive practice and of that of the Reformed tradition, but the immediate decision owed a great deal to the objections of a Hindu convert to Christianity to Brown's practice of praying before a Cross on the wall, which to him seemed compromisingly close to idolatry. Brown was later to claim (with pardonable exaggeration) that, 'my recalcitrant Hindu convert was the man who really put celebrating across the altar into the practice of the world Church'.[6]

As a final example of the kind of innovation pioneered by the CSI, may be cited the placing of the confession and absolution at the opening of the rite: 'I remember the battle fought by Carl Keller of the Basel Mission to have the confession and absolution placed at the beginning of the service on the ground that we needed cleansing to hear the Word aright, as well as rightly to receive the sacrament'.[7] Forty years later an opening penitential rite had become a

[4] Ibid., p. 77.

[5] L. Newbigin, *Unfinished Agenda*, p. 107.

[6] Brown, *Three Worlds*, p. 78.

[7] Newbigin, op. cit., p. 107.

widespread feature of Roman Catholic, Anglican and Protestant eucharistic rites.

The liturgy created by the Committee was first used at the CSI Synod in 1950 and from there spread rapidly within India and beyond. Nor was the creativity of the CSI confined to the eucharist. Daily and Pastoral Offices, the Ordinal and Initiation services were all brought into being in due course, drawing on the same rich background of scholarship, tradition and present need. All have, in various degrees influenced the production of equivalent rites in the different Churches.

As the years have passed, however, some of the strongest criticisms of the CSI rites have come from India itself. Their ready acceptance elsewhere is perhaps a pointer to their lack of a specifically *Indian* character. Brown himself acknowledged this, pointing out that some of the characteristic features, such as the Peace and the anaphoral acclamations, are of Syrian and not Indian origin.[8] 'We still await Indian liturgists, who out of their own understanding of faith and love . . . will be able to produce worship which is Christian through and through but which has its nourishment from India's soul. When they do this, they will have a struggle to get it accepted.' Some of the issues and struggles associated with this new phase of inculturation are discussed in Chapter 15.

It remains to be seen whether the liturgical forms which the Church of South India pioneered and bequeathed to much of the world Church will over time be abandoned in India itself.

[8] Brown, *Three Worlds*, p. 259.

Selected Reading

L. Brown, *Three Worlds, One Word*, London, Rex Collings, 1981.

— *Relevant Liturgy*. London, SPCK, 1965.

T. S. Garret, *Introduction and Comment on the Liturgy of the Church of South India*, Oxford, OUP, 1954.

S. M. Gibbard, 'Liturgical Life in the Church of South India', in *Studia Liturgica*, 3, 1964, pp. 193–210.

L. Newbigin, *Unfinished Agenda*, London, SPCK, 1985.

B. Sundkler, *Church of South India: the Movement Towards Union, 1900–1947*, London, Lutterworth Press, revised edn., 1965.

7

The Roman Catholic Church: From Vatican II to the New Roman Rites 1963–90

The Vatican II Constitution on the Sacred Liturgy

With the calling of the Second Vatican Council by Pope John XXIII (1881–1963), the Roman Catholic Church braced itself for *aggiornamento*. Born Angelo Guiseppe Roncalli near Bergamo (Italy) of peasant parents, he had studied at Bergamo Seminary and was ordained priest in 1905. He served successively as Secretary to the Bishop of Bergamo; an administrator at Rome; Titular Archbishop of Arepolis, living at Sophia and working with Uniat Catholics; Titular Bishop of Mesembria and Apostolic Delegate in Turkey where he established friendly relations with the Orthodox; Papal Nuncio in France; Cardinal and Patriarch in Venice. He was elected Pope in 1958, bringing to that office an ecumenical spirit and a pastoral heart. On 25 January 1959, after only 90 days in office, he announced that he was to call a Synod of the diocese of Rome, an Ecumenical Council to promote Christian unity, and promote a reform of Canon Law. The Council, subsequently to be known as the Second Vatican Council, was formally summoned by the Apostolic Constitution *Humanae Salutis* on 25 December 1961. It was to change the face of the Roman Catholic Church, and equip it for life in the twentieth century. At this stage there was no mention of revision of the liturgy, 'but it was very soon considered a foregone conclusion that it would have to be one of its tasks to occupy itself with the aims of the movement and offer them a timely solution for the Church.'[1]

On 6 June 1960, Cardinal Cicognani was appointed president of the preparatory commission on the liturgy, and on 11 July, Fr Annibale Bugnini CM was appointed secretary. The full commission consisted of sixty-five members and consultors, and about thirty advisers. It included scholars such as Botte, Jungmann and Klauser. The Constitution which they were charged with writing went through a number of drafts. It was announced in October 1962 that the sacred liturgy was the first item on the agenda for examination by the Council Fathers.

Between 1960–62 there was a quick succession of liturgical enactments concerning the Pontifical, Calendar, Missal and Breviary, and some regarded these as an attempt by certain conservatives to pre-empt the Council. If this was the motive, then it failed.

In 1963, before the Council had promulgated any Constitutions, Hans Küng published a set of papers setting out what he (and many others) believed to be the issues and making various suggestions for action.[2] A considerable portion of the book was devoted to liturgical issues, and four in particular stood out for Küng:

1. The use of Latin. Rome recognizes the use of other languages for the liturgy in the Eastern rites, and should now allow the vernacular in the West. Latin impedes the missionary work of the Church, and is not essential to catholicity.

2. The Renewal of the Canon. Küng assumed that in any revision the intercessions or Prayer of the Faithful would be restored. He therefore argued that there was no need to have duplication of intercessions in the canon, and urged a reform of the canon to make clear the

[1] See H. Vorgrimler, *Commentary on the Documents of Vatican II*, London, Burns & Oates, 1967, p. 3.

[2] Hans Küng, *The Council and Reunion*, London, Sheed & Ward, 1963.

main themes of thanksgiving, commemoration and communion.

3. Christian Unity. By a reform of the liturgy Küng hoped that other Churches would be encouraged to seek unity with the Catholic Church. 'If Catholic worship is successfully refashioned in a more ecumenical form, the effect on the whole movement towards reunion with separated Christians will be decisive.'[3]

4. Reform of the Breviary. Küng urged a renewed service of the Word for the entire Christian people; a renewal of monastic hours; and a renewal of prayer for secular priests.

All these were issues which were taken up by the Constitution or in its later implementation, though not all in the way Küng had hoped.

Pope John XXIII did not live to see the work he initiated come to fruition. It was left to his successor, Pope Paul VI, to give the definitive approval and promulgation of the Constitution on the Sacred Liturgy (CSL) on 4 December 1963.

> When the secretary general, Archbishop Felici, announced the results of the vote, his ritual formula was greeted by endlessly prolonged applause that ran from tribune to tribune and throughout the broad naves and vast spaces of the basilica, while a restrained but festive joy was reflected in face after face. 'Holy Father, the Constitution on the Liturgy is acceptable to two thousand one hundred forty-seven Fathers, with four against.' It was an emotional moment, a historical moment.[4]

J. D. Crichton wrote: 'The findings and experiences of the liturgical movement of the last sixty years form the underlying basis of the document and a window is opened on to a future the end of which no man can see.'[5] Indeed, in

[3] Küng, ibid., p. 197.

[4] Bugnini, *Reform*, p. 37.

[5] J. D. Crichton, *The Church's Worship*, London , Geoffrey Chapman, 1964, p. 3.

seven chapters of 130 paragraphs the whole worship of the Roman Catholic Church, more or less frozen since the Council of Trent in the sixteenth century, was put into the melting pot. The introduction and opening sections of the CSL set forth a succinct liturgical theology which was to form the basis of the recommendations for reform. In particular, the following were emphasized:

1. The liturgy enables the faithful to express in their lives and show forth to others the mystery of Christ and the real nature of the Church.

2. In the liturgy we have a foretaste of the heavenly liturgy.

3. While the liturgy is not the whole of the Church's activity, and she must preach the gospel to unbelievers and believers alike, nevertheless 'The liturgy is the summit towards which the activity of the Church is directed; at the same time it is the fount from which all her power flows.' (I.10)

4. In order for this to be achieved, the faithful must take part in its performance intelligently, actively and fruitfully.

In order for this statement to be a reality, the document laid down a series of reforms:

1. There must be instruction in liturgy from university professors in liturgy right through to a pastoral level with instruction of the faithful.

2. The changeable elements in the liturgy can be changed. Changes are to be made to enable people to share in it in a full, active, congregational celebration.

3. Liturgical overgrowth must be removed from the rites. The vernacular must be introduced.

4. More use must be made of Scripture and preaching.

5. The bishop is the centre of an ecclesial community; nevertheless, all Christians have a ministry.

6. Different cultures mean that there will no longer be complete uniformity in all texts and ceremonies. The liturgy may be adapted to the particular genius and traditions of various peoples.

7. The ideal situation is where priests and people share communion; bishops can authorize communion under both kinds.

8. The other sacraments and sacramentals are to be reformed.

9. The Divine Office is to be reformed in such a way as to enable the laity to take part.

10. The liturgical year is to be revised. Saints' days must no longer disrupt the Lord's Day.

11. Above all, the liturgy must be seen to be an important aspect of mission.

12. In music, Gregorian chant still has a special place. However, bishops must make sure that the music is such that the congregation can join in. In the mission fields, traditional music must not be destroyed, but used in liturgy.

13. In the construction of sacred buildings good care must be taken to see that they are designed for the performance of liturgical functions and for the active participation of the faithful.

Underpinning all of this was an implied theology of the Church as the Paschal People of God.

Despite its achievements,

> nobody will conceal the fact that the Constitution also bears the imprints of imperfect human work, both as regards its content and its form. On many questions a middle line had to be drawn between the ideal and tradition, a line which depended upon the momentary balance of rival forces and which resulted in vacillations in the text of the Constitution itself.[6]

[6] Vorgrimler, op. cit., p. 8.

From the Constitution to New Rites

The Constitution on the Sacred Liturgy was a blueprint for revision; now it needed to be implemented. In *motu proprio* of 25 January 1964, *Sacram Liturgiam*, a *Consilium* was set up for the implementation of the CSL, and it also ordered the immediate implementation of certain of the recommendations, particularly seminary teaching of liturgics. The terms of reference of the Consilium were those principles of reform found in paragraphs 21–40 of the CSL. The Consilium consisted of a number of cardinals and bishops, together with consultors – the latter being a team of liturgical scholars who would actually carry out the work. In turn the Consilium was answerable to the Congregation of Rites, and to the Council and Pope. The secretary was Annibale Bugnini, who had already acted as secretary for the preconciliar liturgical reforms. He was to remain secretary to the Consilium and its successor, the Congregation for Divine Worship (1969–75). It is clear that the process of reform was often controversial, with various factions attempting to secure their own particular preferences. Furthermore, there was a conservative backlash which saw the loss of Latin as the loss of a culture. Here public figures from the world of the arts – often with no religious commitment – joined the attack on the reforms. One of the most important groups was Una Voce.[7]

The consultors were assigned particular areas of reform and revision, each group being called *coetus*, headed by a *relator* who would report on the work. Amongst the many liturgical scholars, those of international standing included Balthasar Fischer (relator, baptism), Bernard Botte (ordination), Pierre-Marie Gy (marriage), A-G. Martimort (Divine Office), J. Jungmann, J. Gelineau, L. Bouyer, E. Lengeling, P. Jounel, J. Wagner and C. Vagaggini. (For full details of each coetus or study group, see Bugnini.) Coetus 10 was in

[7] Bugnini, op. cit., Chapter 20.

charge of the Ordinary of the Mass, including the new eucharistic prayers. Coetus 22 was assigned the sacraments and coetus 23 the sacramentals. The Consilium was later to become the Congregation for Divine Worship in 1969, and was renamed the Congregation for Divine Worship and the Discipline of the Sacraments in 1975. Once approved by the Consilium, new texts were reviewed by the Pope and finally issued under his authority by the Congregation. The text then appeared in a Latin *editio typica*, and the work for the Church Universal was complete.

On 29 September 1964, interim instructions were issued to the effect that Mass should be sung on Sundays, a homily should be given, and the laity were to be encouraged to communicate. In May 1967 permission was given for the canon of the Mass to be said aloud. Meanwhile the Consilium worked on the revised and new texts. J. D. Crichton commented:

> At all stages there was widespread consultation and among the members and consultants of the Consilium there were not only liturgical and other scholars but a considerable number of diocesan bishops and priests engaged in pastoral work. In addition . . . various rites were tested in actual pastoral situations and the results were collated for the final redaction of the texts. In this way the laity too have been able to make their needs known.[8]

The following new rites were published: Holy Order (1968), Rite of Funerals (1969), Infant Baptism (1969), Lectionary for the Mass (1969, revised 1981), Marriage (1969), Missal (1970), The Liturgy of the Hours (1971), Confirmation (1971), Christian Initiation of Adults (1972), Lesser Ministries (1972), Anointing of the Sick (1972), Rites of Penance (1973), Dedication of a Church and Altar (1977), Book of Blessings (1984), and Ceremonial for Bishops (1984).

The Apostolic Constitution on the new Missal promulgated by Pope Paul VI began by praising the 1570 Missal,

[8] J. D. Crichton, *The Mass*, London, Geoffrey Chapman, 1971, p. 45; 3rd edn., *Christian Celebration*, p. 53.

and then described the Liturgical Movement as a work of the Holy Spirit and a sign of God's benign providence. It also noted that since 1570 a great deal of study on the ancient and Eastern texts has been carried out:

> Many have expressed the desire that the riches of faith and doctrine contained in these texts should no longer remain hidden in the darkness of library cupboards and shelves, but should be brought out into the light to warm the hearts and enlighten the minds of the Christian peoples.

It also sketched the main features of the new Missal, explaining that the new eucharistic prayers emphasized 'different aspects of the mystery of salvation and to express a variety of motives for giving thanks to God'. The *General Instruction* was published as part of the Altar Missal, giving a commentary on various parts of the Mass, and detailed rubrics. Indeed, each new text was formally issued with an accompanying introduction and instruction explaining the meaning of the rites and giving clear guidance on how they should be used.

ICEL and England

The CSL had given encouragement for the rites to be in the vernacular. It was the task of bishops of the various countries to see that the texts were rendered properly from the Latin into the vernacular. Different countries using the same language were to group together to produce common translations – though this was not always easy, for example, for Spain and the rather different Spanish idiom of Latin American countries. English-speaking areas formed the International Commission on English in the Liturgy (ICEL) in October 1963, having its headquarters in Washington. Its advisory committee first met in Rome in November 1965. Amongst the criteria laid down were the following:

1. The translation must be faithful to the meaning, intention and character of the texts.

2. Respect for the tradition of devotional writing in the English tongue.
3. Contemporary use.
4. Euphony.
5. The practice of other Christian bodies.
6. The language of the middle range of churchgoers.

The procedure was as follows. ICEL produced a draft, a 'green book', which was sent to the bishops. This was duly vetted, and returned for a final 'white book'. When the 'white book' was confirmed by Rome, the texts were then submitted to commercial publishers. However, a further complication arose, since bishops' conferences were not under obligation to use the ICEL versions, and could produce their own translations. This happened in England with the rites of Ordination, Confirmation and the Funeral rites. As a result, some rites have a variety of dates of appearance – the Latin *edition typica*, the ICEL version, and some other versions approved by a bishops' conference. At present ICEL are undertaking fresh translations, which attempt to be faithful to the Latin, but writing in idiomatic English. This new work on the Missal is due to be completed for 1995.

Not everyone has accepted that there should be uniform translations for each linguistic area. In 1984 Canon John McHugh of Ushaw College, in an open letter to the Bishop of Shrewsbury (it was, in fact, a very lengthy paper) called for different styles of English for different areas.

Since the Roman Catholic Church realized that such a revolution in texts and language needed careful instruction and explanation, care has been taken in most First World countries to provide both academic and pastoral studies. In England and Wales the hierarchy have failed to establish an institute (though the Institute for Pastoral Liturgy, Carlow, Eire, can be used), and its pastoral programme for liturgy formation has been rather disorganized. The report *Living Liturgy* (1981) has not been implemented. Books of a substantial nature produced in England have included *The New Liturgy* (1970), *Pastoral Liturgy* (1975), and Edward Matthews' *Celebrating Mass with Children* (1975). In England the National Liturgy Commission is responsible for the bulletin called *Liturgy*. Mention must also be made *Celebration*, a liturgy handbook edited by Stephen Dean, of which the basis is *Celebrating the Paschal Mystery* (1991), which was issued from the National Liturgical Commission for the Conference of Bishops, and is intended to provide a basis for teaching in the parishes.

Selected Reading

W. M. Abbott (ed.), *The Documents of Vatican II*, London, Geoffrey Chapman, 1967.

Bernard Botte, *From Silence to Participation*, Washington, Pastoral Press, 1988.

A. Bugnini, *The Reform of the Liturgy 1948–1975*, Collegeville, Liturgical Press, 1990.

J. D. Crichton, *The Once and the Future Liturgy*, Dublin, Veritas, 1977.

— H. E. Winstone and J. R. Ainslie (eds), *English Catholic Worship*, London, Geoffrey Chapman, 1979.

— *Christian Celebration*, London, Geoffrey Chapman, 1981.

Peter C. Finn and James M. Schellman (eds), *Shaping English Liturgy*, Washington, Pastoral Press, 1990.

E. M. Lengling, 'Protestant Evaluations of the Constitution on the Liturgy', in *Studia Liturgica*, 6 (1969), pp. 3–20.

Living Liturgy. A Report to the Bishops of England and Wales. Slough, St Pauls Publications, 1981.

R. K. Seasoltz, *New Liturgy, New Laws*, Collegeville, Liturgical Press, 1980.

Donald A. Withey, *Catholic Worship. An Introduction to Liturgy*, Rattlesden, Kevin Mayhew, 1990.

8
The Anglican Church and the Liturgical Movement II

Lambeth 1958

The Report on *The Book of Common Prayer* of the 1958 Lambeth Conference marked the beginning of a great deal of liturgical revision throughout the Anglican Communion. The Report stressed the primacy of worship in the life of the Church, and the place of the Prayer Book in the life of the Anglican Communion. It also suggested the recovery of 'primitive' elements which had fallen out (e.g. at the eucharist, the use of an Old Testament lesson, and in the eucharistic prayer, thanksgiving for the mighty works of God) and fuller participation of the laity (e.g. the restoration of the prayers of the people). Dr Leslie Brown, now Archbishop of Uganda, who had been the prime drafter of the CSI liturgy (see Chapter 6) was secretary of the sub-committee which prepared the report, and as Ronald Jasper has remarked, 'It is not surprising to find its eucharistic proposals to be a virtual endorsement of the structure of the CSI liturgy'.[1]

A Liturgy for Africa

Conceived in Kampala in April 1961, *A Liturgy for Africa* was drafted there in April 1963 at a meeting with representatives of a number of African Anglican Provinces. Leslie Brown was responsible for much of the work, submitting it to four

[1] Jasper, *Development*, p. 215.

members of the Church of England Liturgical Commission for comment. The definitive text was published in 1964. As might be expected, this eucharistic liturgy was in direct succession with CSI and the proposals of Lambeth 1958.

The 'Pan-Anglican' documents

These were prepared in order to give some further guidance for the revision of Anglican liturgies in the hope of achieving some sort of family conformity. The first dates from 1965, being the work of Archbishops Leslie Brown and H. H. Clark, Bishop C. K. Sainsbury and Professor Massey Shepherd Jr of the American Episcopal Church. It was concerned with the eucharist, and gave a recommended common structure. A revision of this document was undertaken by Leslie Brown (by now Bishop of St Edmundsbury and Ipswich in England) and Dr Ronald Jasper, the Chairman of the Church of England Liturgical Commission. It was published in 1969 under the title *The Structure and Contents of the Eucharistic Liturgy and the Daily Office*.

Official English revision to 1967

Most provinces of the Anglican Communion embarked upon liturgical revision. England has been used as an example of the type of process involved, though in other provinces the procedure was often simpler. The Church of England Liturgical Commission had been involved in the preparation of the Lambeth report on the Prayer Book; it had also turned its attention to the question of baptism, and in 1959 produced a report entitled *Baptism and Confirmation*. The full rite of Adult Baptism, Confirmation and Holy Communion was to be the archetypal service, and other services were adapted from it. Opposition to the proposed forms came from a member of the Commission, Dean Milner-White of York, and ultimately the report was rejected as being too radical.

In 1964 Archbishop Michael Ramsey reshaped the Commission, and with Ronald Jasper as chairman, it was set on a course which was ultimately to give birth to the 1980 *Alternative Service Book* (ASB). A number of important events can be singled out in the period until 1967:

1. The first necessity was to clear the legal ground to prevent a repetition of 1928. In 1964 the Vestments of Ministers Measure was passed, getting rid of doctrinal significance of vesture. (Ever since the second-generation Tractarians of the nineteenth century, the use of the traditional Western eucharistic vestments, particularly the chasuble, had been seen by Evangelicals as a Roman badge symbolizing the sacrifice of the Mass, whereas the wearing of the surplice, scarf and hood for the eucharist was seen by High Churchmen as indicating an extreme Protestant and 'Zwinglian' concept of the eucharist. Now only the perverse could object to any type of vesture other than on purely personal sartorial grounds.) In 1965 the Prayer Book (Alternative and other Services) Measure was passed which allowed the Church to authorize its own services without recourse to Parliament.

2. In 1965 a number of services called Series 1 were brought forward for consideration. They were mainly material from the 1928 Prayer Book which was popularly in use. After discussion and emendation the Series 1 Alternative Services were authorized from 1966 for two years.

3. Services were published in December 1965 as *Alternative Services Second Series*. This book of services was a report containing Morning and Evening Prayer, Intercessions and Thanksgivings, Thanksgiving after Childbirth, Burial of the Dead, and a new Order for Holy Communion. Some of these services represented a radical re-structuring, and were new compositions. The most striking was the Holy Communion, where Prayer Book forms had been blended with the structure of Justin

Martyr and phraseology from Hippolytus's *Apostolic Tradition*. The draft order contained the words 'we offer unto thee this bread and this cup' in the eucharistic prayer, which resulted in controversy, and dissent from the report by Colin Buchanan, an Evangelical member of the Liturgical Commission. An emended text was finally authorized in July 1967. The Burial Service was never authorized. Baptism and Confirmation were published in 1967, and authorized in 1968.

Official English revision 1967–80

All the Series 1 and 2 services were written in mock Tudor–Stuart language, and harmonized with the language of the Prayer Book. In 1967 the Liturgical Commission had published *Modern Liturgical Texts*, which presented certain texts in modern English. It became clear that while most English-speaking Churches were composing rites in mock seventeenth-century language, the Roman Catholic ICEL was, with the exception of the Lord's Prayer, going to use modern vernacular English rather than some form of sacred English. It seemed sensible to have some standard texts across the denominations, and out of ICEL in 1968 was born ICET (The International Consultation on English Texts). In 1970 a collection of common texts appeared in a booklet called *Prayers We Have in Common*. The Church of England always felt free to revise these texts, and did so in its own modern version of the Lord's Prayer. However, as a result of these developments, nearly all revision after 1967 was in modern English. It became obvious that, like 'man born of woman', Series 1 and 2 had but a short time to live. (In fact, the eucharistic rites continued to be legal until 31 December 1980 and 31 December 1985 respectively.) A new Series, Series 3, appeared and it was these services which were to form the core of the ASB 1980. Important landmarks include:

1. In 1971 Series 3 Order of Holy Communion (in a white cover) was issued. It was revised and authorized from 1973. It was followed by Series 3 Collects, Initiation, Marriage, Burial and Ordination – though the latter was never printed in authorized form as a separate booklet, but appeared in final form in the ASB.

2. In 1973 the Commission worked on a symposium called *The Eucharist Today*, which was a series of essays in defence of the Series 3 eucharistic liturgy.

3. In 1974 the Church of England (Worship and Doctrine) Measure was passed, superseding the Alternative Services Measure and other older legislation, most notably the Act of Uniformity 1662. It left the text of the 1662 Prayer Book in the custody of Parliament, but devolved to the General Synod the authority to make changes in all other liturgical matters.

4. The ASB finally appeared in November 1980. It evoked a Pastoral Letter from the Archbishops of Canterbury and York, which the clergy were asked to regard as confidential until a certain date. The late Douglas Webb aptly commented: 'It was a letter of such inconsequence that it could have remained confidential for ever without any great loss.' In spite of criticism from certain opponents of any form of revision, the Church in general gladly received the new book. Ronald Jasper commented: 'The new book has broken a mould which had survived for three and a half centuries, and it has done so by a process of supplementation.'[2]

Scholars, drafters, exponents and opponents

Amongst Commission members over the years from 1964 to 1980, a number of names stand out as being instrumental in the drafting of the new services. In the early days the

[2] *Development*, p. 360.

Commission lost E. C. Ratcliff through death, and A. H. Couratin resigned over the changes made to the Series 2 eucharistic prayer. G. G. Willis (1914–82) had to resign on account of blindness. However, Ronald Jasper (1917–90), an able historian who was Reader in Liturgy at King's College, London, and Geoffrey Cuming (1917–88) who became part-time lecturer at King's College, London and was already a distinguished scholar of the Anglican liturgical tradition, more than made up for these losses. Colin Buchanan (1934–) who joined to represent the Conservative Evangelicals, made a steadily increasing contribution, and Charles Whittaker (1916–88) had published a number of studies on the rites of baptism.

Although the Church itself put out one or two small booklets to explain liturgical revision, and to present some of the new services, it lacked anything like the French Centre de Liturgie Pastoral or the Institut Supérieur de Liturgie. It was fortunate to have the liturgical scholars it did have, since it had no programme in its theological colleges or universities for training people in this complex discipline. Mention must be made of the Institute of Worship and Architecture at Birmingham, which did provide academic and pastoral support for liturgical renewal in the 1960s and early 1970s; indeed, its Director, Professor J. G. Davies, and two associates, Gilbert Cope and Donald Tytler, had pioneered an *Experimental Liturgy* in 1958, which reflected the thinking of CSI and the Lambeth Conference. Later this Institute tended to subside into sociological studies, and on the retirement of Professor Davies, was closed. However, it is probably Colin Buchanan with Grove Liturgical Studies and *News of Liturgy* who has done more than anyone in England to stimulate liturgical discussion and give it practical, pastoral application.

Inevitably, not everyone greeted the new services with enthusiasm. The Prayer Book Society was formed to promote the use and study of the *Book of Common Prayer*, and attacked the new services on literary grounds. Extreme

Evangelical attacks included a booklet by D. A. Scales, *What Mean Ye by This Service?* (1969) which attacked the Series 2 Communion as a sell-out to Roman Catholicism (the booklet was written in the style of sixteenth-century polemic, and betrays a total lack of liturgical scholarship), and the more scholarly work of R. T. Beckwith and J. E. Tiller, *The Service of Holy Communion and its Revision* (1972). Attacks from the extreme Anglo-Catholic wing included the pamphlets by G. G. Willis, *1966 and All That* (1969), and M. Moreton, *Made Fully Perfect* (1974), both alleging that the new Communion rites were a sell-out to Protestantism. (See Chapter 16 for further criticism.)

Revision since 1980

A new Liturgical Commission was appointed in 1981 under the chairmanship of Canon Douglas Jones. It worked on a major compilation, *Lent, Holy Week, and Easter* which appeared at the end of 1984. It also provided services of prayer to be used after a Civil Marriage: Geoffrey Cuming served as a consultant, as did Michael Perham, the secretary to the Doctrine Commission. The latter, together with Trevor Lloyd and Dr Paul Bradshaw, did much of the drafting of the new texts. An almost completely new Commission was appointed in 1986 under chairmanship of the Bishop of Winchester, the Rt. Revd Colin James. Figures such as Colin Buchanan and Donald Gray were 'retired', and Dr Paul Bradshaw, a noted liturgical scholar, had resigned on taking up a university appointment in the USA. Part of the brief of this new Commission was to enrich the ASB which was felt to be bare in places, and in need of more variety. This new Commission produced two major compilations: *Patterns for Worship*, which provided material for use at Family Services and in Urban Priority Areas; and *The Promise of His Glory*, containing material from Advent to Candlemas. Drafters included Michael Perham, Trevor Lloyd, Dr Kenneth Stevenson and Dr Bryan Spinks, David Stancliffe and David

Silk. The subsequent Commission of 1991 was little changed, except the 'retirement' of David Silk and Geoffrey Rowell, but with the addition of the distinguished novelist, Baroness James (P. D. James), a Vice-President of the Prayer Book Society. Part of the brief of this Commission is to report on the changes thought necessary to the ASB, which is authorized only until the year 2000.

The Anglican Communion

The days are long gone when the Anglican Church was synonymous with the Church of England. The American Episcopal Church began a series of 'Prayer Book Studies' which paved the way for revision. Beginning in the 1950s, these were able to give textual expression to the insights of the Liturgical Movement. The final outcome of the many experimental texts was a new Prayer Book in 1979. As we have seen, *A Liturgy for Africa* also anticipated any English revision. The collections of C. O. Buchanan, *Modern Anglican Liturgies 1958–1968*, *Further Anglican Liturgies 1968–1975* and *Latest Anglican Liturgies 1986–1984* give some idea of the plethora of liturgical rites which have been produced between 1958 and 1984. The general pattern has been to issue experimental services leading to a new Prayer Book. Smaller provinces, particular those in the Third World, which lack expertise and resources to undertake fresh revision, often adopted or adapted the English or American material. Notable Prayer Books appearing recently include those of the Church of Ireland (1984), Canada (1985), South Africa (1989) and New Zealand (1989). Those of the Church of Ireland and South Africa show a certain dependence upon the English ASB, though by no means without their own respective adaptations and new material. The South African eucharistic rite included one of the new Roman Catholic eucharistic prayers for authorized use. The Canadian book is an extremely rich collection, though using a considerable amount of material from the American book of 1979. Perhaps the most innovative is the New Zealand book. It omits all reference to Israel and deliberately reflects its Pacific cultural setting, particularly the Maori culture.[3]

Selected Reading

T. G. A. Baker, *Questioning Worship*, London, SCM, 1977.

C. O. Buchanan (ed.), *Modern Anglican Liturgies 1958–1968*, Oxford, OUP, 1968.

— *Recent Liturgical Revision in the Church of England*, Grove Booklet on Ministry and Worship 14, Bramcote, Grove Books, 1973. *Supplements* 14A (1974), 14B (1976), 14C (1978).

— *Further Anglican Liturgies 1968–1975*, Bramcote, Grove Books, 1975.

— *Latest Liturgical Revision in the Church of England 1978–1984*, Grove Liturgical Study 39, Bramcote, Grove Books, 1984.

— *Latest Anglican Liturgies 1976–1984*, London, Alcuin Club/SPCK, 1985.

R. C. D. Jasper (ed.), *The Eucharist Today*, London, SPCK, 1974.

— *The Development of the Anglican Liturgy 1662–1980*, London, SPCK, 1989.

M. Perham (ed.), *The Renewal of Common Prayer*, London, Church House/SPCK, 1993.

Bosco Peters, *The Anglican Eucharist in New Zealand 1814–1989*, Alcuin/GROW Liturgical Study 21, Bramcote, Grove Books, 1992.

[3] A good summary and discussion of the New Zealand book by Trevor Lloyd is to be found in *News of Liturgy* 182, February 1990, pp. 3–6.

9

The Liturgical Movement in the English Reformed and Methodist Churches

In both the British Reformed and Methodist traditions the Liturgical Movement has been at work. However, unlike the Roman Catholic and Anglican Churches, these traditions do not have a compulsory liturgy, and some sections of these Churches make a point of not following set prayers. As a result the impact of the movement is less easy to trace, and the extent of its influence difficult to assess.

The Reformed tradition

Nineteenth-century activity

The British Reformed tradition has been represented by two main groupings; the Presbyterians, who have long been the Established Church in Scotland, but whose influence in England reached a peak between 1640–58, and thereafter declined; and the Congregationalists, who surfaced as a vocal minority in the 1640s, and who gradually increased in numbers to become the major Reformed force in England. Scottish and English Presbyterianism inherited the English adaptations of Calvin's Genevan liturgy, which was regarded as a guide for the minister rather than an invariable text which the congregation could follow. In 1644 the *Westminster Directory* had been adopted (replacing the Anglican *Book of Common Prayer* in England) which simply gave an outline of the services with guides to the content of the various prayers and exhortations. In practice most ministers practised extempore prayer. The Congregationalists (or Independents as they were formerly called) had assisted in the compilation of the *Westminster Directory*, but tended to argue that one of the gifts of the Spirit to those called to the ministry was the ability to pray extempore. This wing of the Reformed tradition tended to be anti-liturgical in terms of written texts.

The nineteenth century witnessed a reawakening of interest in liturgical forms in the Reformed tradition generally. Of particular importance was the Liturgy of the Catholic Apostolic Church, which combined a Reformed background with a pentecostal fervour, and a very Catholic liturgy. Although the eschatological stance of this Church, and its Catholic ceremonial, made it a cause for suspicion amongst other Reformed Churches, its liturgy, *The Liturgy and other Divine Offices of the Church*, did exert an influence, and it 'remains as a permanent testimony of its life and teaching, and a little-understood legacy to liturgical history'.[1]

The Mercersburg Movement in the German Reformed tradition in America combined dogmatics with liturgical research, and its leaders relied heavily on the Catholic Apostolic liturgy for their Provisional Liturgy of 1857.[2] In turn, some Church of Scotland ministers who founded the Church Service Society to promote good worship, and investigate liturgical traditions of the past, drew on both the Mercersburg liturgy and that of the Catholic Apostolic Church in the *Euchologion* of 1867. Through subsequent editions of the *Euchologion*, and its more general concern for worship, the Church Service Society influenced future liturgical revision in the Church of Scotland, culminating in the 1940 *Book of Common Order*. This in turn influenced English Reformed groups.

[1] See K. W. Stevenson, 'The Catholic Apostolic Church – its History and its Eucharist', *Studia Liturgica*, 13 (1979) 21–43.

[2] J. M. Maxwell, *Worship and Reformed Theology – The Liturgical Lessons of Mercersburg*, Pittsburg, 1976.

The United Reformed Church: liturgical background before 1972

The United Reformed Church came about by Act of Parliament in 1972, and brought together the Congregational Church in England and Wales (formerly the Congregational Union of England and Wales) and the Presbyterian Church of England (which mainly evolved from nineteenth-century Scottish settlers in England).

The Presbyterian Church of England was the smaller of the two uniting bodies. It had a number of liturgies put out for the use of ministers – *Directory for the Public Worship of God* (1894), *Directory for Public Worship* (1898), and, under the influence of the 1940 Scottish liturgy, *The Presbyterian Service Book* (1948). Individuals have also published liturgies privately, for example W. E. Orchard's *Service Book* at Enfield *c.* 1912. A new liturgy appeared in 1968, but it was extremely conservative, and not too different in character from the 1948 liturgy. The convener of the Presbyterian Committee on Public Worship and Aids to Devotion admitted that the revision had taken far too long, and was already out of date when it appeared: 'Now we had little pride in it and watched its emergence with relief rather than gratitude.'[3]

The situation in Congregationalism was more interesting. Some Congregationalists had already started to use liturgical forms in the nineteenth century. Some of these were compiled for affluent congregations, and were based on the *Book of Common Prayer*. However, a great pioneer in liturgical forms which were influential among Congregationalists was John Hunter in his various editions of *Devotional Services*. Less influential were the maverick High Church liturgies produced by W. E. Orchard when he was nominally a Congregationalist. He compiled a liturgy using Eastern and Roman Catholic sources, and celebrated the

[3] Norman Leak, 'Recent Developments in Public Worship and Aids to Devotion – Presbyterian Church of England', *Liturgical Review*, 3 (1973), 26–31, p. 26.

eucharist using Catholic ceremonial and vestments. The Congregational Union on behalf of the denomination produced a liturgy in 1920, and the committee producing it had included P. T. Forsyth, 'a Barthian before Barth', though there is no hint of his strong sacramentalism and ecclesiology in this liturgy.

In the 1930s, Congregationalism was heavily influenced by Liberal Protestantism, and the 1936 liturgy issued on behalf of the denomination, under the Chairmanship of John Phillips, *A Manual for Ministers*, represented such a theology. However, in the very same year as the publication of this Liberal Protestant liturgy, there appeared from the Oxford University Press a collection of essays edited by Nathaniel Micklem of Mansfield College, Oxford, entitled *Christian Worship*. The Foreword claimed that the collection was 'A systematic study of Public Worship' and expressed the hope that the historical studies would be accepted as a serious contribution to the subject, and that the later chapters would serve as an interpretation and a vindication of the common traditions of the Reformed Churches. The essays included biblical, historical and contemporary studies. Professor Horton Davies commented: 'Apart from its intrinsic importance, the volume was a portent.'[4] Indeed, it was a portent; in the 1940s Barthianism and the continental Liturgical Movement resulted in a movement back to Calvinist and Patristic roots. A group called the Church Order Group was set up, and disseminated its views through a journal called *The Presbyter*. Four members of this 'Genevan' group – John Marsh, John Huxtable, James Todd and Nathaniel Micklem – edited a liturgy entitled *A Book of Public Worship*, which was published by the Oxford University Press in 1948. This book offered a rich, orthodox collection of worship, drawing on the classical Reformed tradition, and the early liturgies. A companion volume, *Services for Christian Festivals* was published by Todd in 1951. The denominational press, the

[4] H. Davies, *Worship and Theology in England 1900–1965*, Princeton University Press, 1962, p. 45.

Independent Press, had declined to publish the 1948 volume. However, the influence and popularity of these two books, which reflected the principles of the Liturgical Movement, is seen in the denomination liturgy of 1959, *A Book of Services and Prayers*, which abandoned the earlier Liberal Protestant stance, and reflected the 'Genevan' and Patristic flavour of the 1948 and 1951 books.

Two important books produced by Congregationalists were Horton Davies' *The Worship of the English Puritans* (1948), reminding his denomination that it did possess a liturgical tradition; and Raymond Abba's *Principles of Christian Worship* (1957), which presented the principles of the Liturgical Movement in a Congregationalist context.

Two important books were published in the 1960s. An official communion service was begun in 1964 by the Liturgical Group (subsequently to become the Liturgical Committee in 1966, and the Worship Committee in 1967). It was completed in 1967, but because of delays *An Order of Public Worship* did not appear until 1970. The principle persons involved were James Todd, Dr John Huxtable, Dr John Gregory and Stuart Gibbons. Gibbons had studied liturgy at Oxford under the Anglican liturgist, A. H. Couratin. However, the book was in Tudor–Stuart language, and by 1970 it was obvious that the rite would be little used. The influence of liturgical scholarship is seen in the fact that out of six eucharistic prayers, three ended with the Sanctus in a manner suggested by Ratcliff and Couratin as being the original ending of the anaphora of Hippolytus's *Apostolic Tradition*.

In 1967 *Contemporary Prayers for Christian Worship* had been published by SCM Press. This was the work of five younger Congregational ministers, and being in modern English, was quite influential.

United Reformed Church: 1972–90

In response to the WCC 1968 Uppsala Report on Worship, both the Presbyterian Committee on Public Worship and

Aids to Devotion, and the Congregational Church's Worship Committee had published some discussion papers in 1971, entitled respectively *Symposium on Worship* and *About Worship*. However, with the formation of the United Reformed Church, a Worship and Doctrine Committee was appointed, and immediately charged with drawing up new orders for worship in the new united denomination. Orders were compiled for experimental use, under the successive chairmanships of Dr Eric Routley, the noted musician, Dr John Huxtable and Dr B. Johanson. First was the Ordination and Induction of Elders 1973, then the Order of Worship (eucharist) 1974, and Initiation in 1976. All services were completed by 1978, though some were never published as separate services. The eucharist of 1974 was published with a musical setting in 1975 in *New Church Praise*, giving Reformed churchmen a liturgy in their hands as well as a hymn book. The final *A Book of Services* was issued in 1980.

In 1985 the General Assembly of the URC decided that the 1980 book was already in need of revision. Two important reasons were the move towards the use of inclusive language, and the fact that in 1981 the Reformed Association of Churches of Christ in Great Britain and Ireland came into the URC. The liturgical traditions of the Churches of Christ needed to be amalgamated and incorporated within the URC liturgies. A new Doctrine and Worship Committee was appointed under Colin Gunton as convener. Drafters included Charles Brock of Mansfield College, and from the former Churches of Christ, Dr David Thompson of the Divinity Faculty, Cambridge University. The Anglican liturgist, Bryan Spinks, was a corresponding consultant. The new *Service Book* was published at the end of 1989.

It should be understood, however, that no URC minister is obliged to use any of the officially published rites, and many do not. David Owen's book, *Sharers in Worship* (1980), gives another side of the liturgical renewal in the URC; practical tips for dignified services, together with insights from modern educational techniques have played as much part, if not more, than the official texts. *Partners in Learning* has been an important influence on developing the Family Church concept. Also popular with ministers in some areas are the services by Alan Gaunt published by John Paul the Preachers' Press: *New Prayers for Worship* (1972) and subsequently in four stages *Prayers for the Christian Year*.

The Methodist Church

The 1936 Book of Offices

John Wesley combined the use of extempore prayer and preaching services (probably developed from the Oxford University Sermon tradition) with a high esteem for the *Book of Common Prayer*, and had made an abridgement of the latter in 1784. In Wesleyan Methodism various editions of the Abridgement continued to appear, though some ministers simply used the 1662 Prayer Book. However, other Methodist groups espoused free prayer, and despised liturgical forms. In the nineteenth century some of these groups did issue forms of service for the guidance of the minister. For example, the Primitive Methodists issued forms in 1860 and *c.* 1890; the Bible Christians produced *Service Book* in 1903, and the United Methodists produced a liturgy in 1913.[5] When the various Methodist traditions in England came together to unite in 1932, there were a number of very different liturgical traditions. The United Church issued *The Book of Offices* in 1936, which was heavily indebted to the Prayer Books of 1662 and 1928, and was not used by all of the groups within the United Church.

Signs of a Liturgical Movement

In 1936 J. Ernest Rattenbury published *Vital Elements of Public Worship*. Rattenbury, a noted historian of the

[5] J. C. Bowmer, articles in *Proceedings of the Wesleyan Historical Society*, 32 and 33 (1960–62).

Methodist tradition, explored the ingredients of good worship, urging dignity, gravity and order in Methodist services. It represented a strong defence of liturgical forms, and emphasized the corporate nature of Christian worship.

Another sign of liturgical renewal was in the formation of the Methodist Sacramental Fellowship in 1935. It was founded by a group of young ministers who were distressed by the growing irreverence of many Methodist services, and the prevailing liberalism. It emphasized the corporate nature of the Church, sacramental devotion, recital of the Daily Office, and reception of communion at least once a month. It mediated the insights of the continental Liturgical Movement, and drew attention to the rich eucharistic theology of Wesley's hymns.

Perhaps one of the most notable literary signs of the influence of the Liturgical Movement was to be found in J. C. Bowmer's *The Lord's Supper in Methodism 1791–1960*, published in 1961. Concluding his historical survey, Bowmer made the following conclusions, taking into account modern scholarship:

1. There was no need for Methodists to cling to the 1662 Prayer Book.

2. The Communion order should be an act of corporate worship. There should be more congregational responses, and *An Experimental Liturgy* (1958) and the *Liturgy of South India* were good examples for Methodists to take note of.

3. Methodists should not be afraid of ceremonial.

4. There should be more regular use of the full service of Holy Communion.

5. Before any revision, experimental services should be practised.

6. The individual cups used by Methodists should be replaced by the common cup.

7. Methodist architecture should change accordingly, and have a free-standing communion table.

8. There should be more teaching about the Lord's Supper from the pulpit.

Bowmer, writing in 1960/61 had the advantage of being party to the Report made in 1960 to the Methodist Conference urging that the time had come for new services, and orders should be prepared for a period of experimentation.

The Methodist Service Book 1975

In 1961 the Methodist Conference asked the Faith and Order Committee to investigate the desirability of revising the Book of Offices of 1936. In 1962 the *London Quarterly and Holborn Review* carried four articles designed to pave the way for that revision, and in the same year Conference resolved, on receiving the report of the Faith and Order Committee, that:

> the Book of Offices be revised over a period of years; that the baptismal services and the service for the Public Reception of New Members be considered first; that a draft revision of these services be prepared and submitted to a future conference with a view to experimental use; and that the Faith and Order Committee be authorized to co-opt suitable people on to a sub-committee to prepare such a draft.

In March 1963 a Methodist Liturgical Conference was held at Didsbury College, Bristol, and important articles on worship appeared in the *London Quarterly and Holborn Review* in 1963 and 1964. Important names associated with the preparatory work and drafting include Raymond George, Gordon Wakefield, Rupert Davies, David Tripp and Geoffrey Wainwright. An example of the Liturgical Movement being brought to the attention of Methodism, and perhaps also an attempt to influence the course of the revision was Raymond Billington's *The Liturgical Movement and Methodism* (1969). This work was originally an MA thesis for Queen's College, Birmingham, and the book was published after some of the new services had already appeared.

The course of revision was as follows:

1967 – the Baptismal Services and Public Reception into Full Membership, or Confirmation.

1968 – The Sunday Service, and the Burial or Cremation of the Dead.

1969 – The Covenant Service.

1970 – The Marriage Service.

Certain other services were to be compiled, but were not to be included in the final service book, though it would be understood that they enjoyed the same status. In 1969 another committee had been preparing collects, lessons and psalms, and they made great use of the Joint Liturgical Group's calendar and lectionary, the additional lectionary and the Daily Office (see below). The 1968 Sunday Service was issued in parallel texts – a mock Tudor–Stuart version, and a contemporary English version. All later revisions were in contemporary English. The services were approved by Conference in 1974, and together with 'The Ordination of ministers also called Presbyters', based on the Anglican–Methodist proposed Ordinal, they appeared as *The Methodist Service Book* in 1975.

According to the review by Geoffrey Wainwright in the *Epworth Review* (1976), the new service book reflected the concerns of the Liturgical, Pastoral and Ecumenical Movements, and R. C. D. Jasper felt it was faithful to the ecumenical approaches to worship. However, Professor Gordon Rupp, the noted historian, fiercely attacked the book in the *Epworth Review* (1981). He disagreed with the attempt to make the normative service in Methodism a eucharist; it should have paid more attention to the Methodist 'hymn-sandwich' (did he not mean 'Preaching Service'?) and felt that there was too much regard for the period between the fourth and sixth centuries, and too little attention given to the Protestant liturgical tradition.

Quite separately the Youth Department published orders for Family Worship in 1971, and the Methodist Sacramental Fellowship published orders for daily Morning and Evening Prayer.

Formation and revision

An important discussion document and guide for worship was the Report of the 1988 Methodist Conference's Commission on Worship, entitled *Let the People Worship*. Among its recommendations for discussion at congregational level were more involvement of lay people in worship, and an emphasis on two intentions of worship: adoration of God and allowing God to transform the worshippers. At the same time it welcomed the revision of the 1975 service book which is currently in progress.

Other bodies and the Joint Liturgical Group

North of the Border the Church of Scotland revised its 1940 *Book of Common Order* with a new book of the same title in 1979. A further revision of the same title appeared on Ascension Day 1994. One notable feature of this latter was use of material from the French Reformed Church in the rite of baptism.

A small group of conservative churchmen who regarded the 1940 and 1979 books as representing 'Scoto-Catholicism', published in 1977 the *Reformed Book of Common Order* which is a quaint attempt to prune Knox's sixteenth-century liturgy of High Calvinism.

The Baptist Union has refrained from publishing official orders for its ministers. An important collection by E. A. Payne and S. F. Winward, *Orders and Prayers for Church Worship*, was published in 1960. Another collection by Alec Gilmore, Edward Smalley and Michael Walker entitled *Praise God: A Collection of Material for Christian Worship* was published by the Baptist Union in 1980. Most recently the denomination has produced *Patterns and Prayers for Christian Worship* (1992), published by the Oxford University Press.

Just as through colonialism Anglicanism spread beyond the British Isles, so too English nonconformity has been exported to many parts of the world. The pattern outlined for Great Britain can be paralleled elsewhere such as in Canada, parts of Africa and Australia and New Zealand. It should be remembered, however, that in the Reformed, Methodist and Baptist traditions these liturgies are only a guide for the minister, and many make little use of them, and still rely on free or extempore prayer.

A number of the British Reformed and Nonconformist Churches have participated in the British ecumenical liturgical body called the Joint Liturgical Group (JLG). In 1963, at the instigation of R. C. D. Jasper, the Archbishop of Canterbury invited participation of eight Churches in England, Scotland and Wales, under the chairmanship of Dean Douglas Harrison. The Roman Catholics were originally observers, but have since become full members. The aim of the Group was set out as follows:

> 1. The planning of a Calendar, Forms of Daily Service, and a Lectionary which the Churches might be glad to have in common.
>
> 2. The planning of joint forms of service which might be used with the approval of the several Churches on occasions for united worship such as the Week of Prayer for Christian Unity and Holy Week.
>
> 3. The consideration of the structure of the service of Holy Communion.

Publications have included the Daily Office, the structure of initiation and the eucharist, a eucharistic prayer, essays on *Getting the Liturgy Right*, and most recently, *A Word in Season* and *A Four Year Lectionary*. Perhaps the most influential books have been *The Calendar and Lectionary* (1967) and *The Daily Office* (1968, revised 1978).

Selected Reading

J. M. Barkley, *The Worship of the Reformed Church*, London, Lutterworth Press, 1966.

R. J. Billington, *The Liturgical Movement and Methodism*, London, Epworth Press, 1969.

J. C. Bowmer, *The Lord's Supper in Methodism 1791–1960*, London, Epworth Press, 1961.

Adrian Burdon, *The Preaching Service – The Glory of the Methodists*, Alcuin/GROW Liturgical Study 17, Bramcote, 1991.

A. R. George, 'The Changing Face of Methodism I: The Methodist Service Book', in *Proceedings of the Wesley Historical Society*, 41 (1977), pp. 65–72.

David Owen, *Sharers in Worship*, Redhill, NCEC, 1980.

Bryan D. Spinks, *Freedom or Order? The Eucharistic Liturgy in English Congregationalism 1645–1980*, Alison Park, Pickwick Publications, 1984.

James F. White, *Protestant Worship*, Louisville, Kentucky, Westminster/John Knox Press, 1989.

10

The Eastern Churches and the Liturgical Movement

The relationship between the Orthodox and Oriental Churches and the Liturgical Movement is a complex one. The designation 'Orthodox' is commonly used for the family of Churches in communion with the Patriarch of Constantinople and each other – Greece, Russia, Romania, Serbia, Bulgaria, etc. The Oriental Orthodox Churches are those of Armenia, Syria, Egypt, Ethiopia and India. The two families have been formally separated since the Council of Chalcedon in AD 451 but have in recent decades gone a long way to patching up the doctrinal differences between them. They share a common approach to worship and for the purposes of this chapter may be regarded as a single – though diverse – family. At first glance these Eastern Churches have hardly, if at all, been affected by the Liturgical Movement. Yet many pioneers of the Liturgical Movement would testify that it was the worship of the Orthodox Churches which provided the inspiration for their reforming work. Indeed, the Orthodox Churches of the East have, through a variety of routes, had a marked impact upon the development of the Liturgical Movement, which owes its origins in part at least to a rediscovery of the East and of the insights of the early Church preserved by the East and lost by the West. Since the separation of East and West, the isolation of the Western Church from the rest of Christianity allowed the growth of monolithic Roman Catholicism immune from the insights available from other strands of Christian tradition. Local liturgical traditions were gradually suppressed and the Roman rite universally imposed.

In contrast, the Eastern Churches preserved a degree of liturgical variety, reflecting their ethnic diversity and the absence of any one Patriarch accorded anything like the supremacy of the Bishop of Rome in the West. The worship of the East preserves a degree of mysticism and an awareness of the unceasing worship of heaven which was largely alien to Western rationality. The Orthodox also retain specific rites and insights of the early Church lost in the West.

The Reformation in the West in the sixteenth century provided a potential point of fresh contact. In practice little developed, the Reformers' central concern of justification by faith not being so prominent in the East. However, Cranmer borrowed 'the prayer of St Chrysostom', which may well indicate some knowledge of the Orthodox. Negatively, reaction to the Reformation led to the Counter-Reformation in the Roman Church and the growth of private piety and private Masses; the insight of the East would later be a cause of the demise of such trends.

In rediscovering the East, the Liturgical Movement found a point of contact with the continuing worship of the Church which avoided the extremes of Western medievalism. In addition, insights were retained which came afresh to the modern mind and had not been part of the ongoing debates between Catholic and Protestant. Central insights included the regular celebration of the eucharist by the whole community. In Roman Catholic piety the Mass had been celebrated repeatedly in private or with laity as spectators at major celebrations. Many Protestant Churches had almost lost the celebration of the eucharist altogether. In contrast, the eucharist in the East was for the whole people, not a private affair between the priest and God, and never attracted the quasi-mechanical association with the winning of grace and merit which it did in the Latin Church.

The bishop as a liturgical figure remained important in the East whereas Western developments had left him in an administrative and social role. The epiclesis, calling down the Spirit upon the elements, presented a vital insight into the spiritual dynamic of the eucharist, in stark contrast to the near-mechanical working of the priestly recitation of the words of institution in the Western rite. In addition, there was a flavour to Eastern worship – in particular an emphasis upon the resurrection and glory rather than upon the piety of the suffering of Christ of the West – which, although hard to quantify, preserved an atmosphere of *celebration* which became increasingly significant for the Liturgical Movement.

It is extraordinary how many involved in the Liturgical Movement owe at least some of their thinking to Eastern contacts. Pope John XXIII served as a papal diplomat in Istanbul and encountered a liturgical tradition very different in many ways to that of Italy. Advocates of reform in the Roman Catholic Church prior to Vatican II could point to the Eastern-rite Catholic (Uniat) Churches within the Roman fold as evidence that the Latin tradition was not the only valid Catholic one. This fact undoubtedly made easier the acceptance of some of the liturgical reforms following Vatican II. In addition, the influx of thousands of Russians and Greeks into Western Europe and North America following the Bolshevik Revolution and the expulsion of the Greeks from Turkey made Orthodox worship much more easily accessible to Western Christians. The example of Lambert Beauduin is perhaps illustrative of the significance of this contact and influence. Beauduin had experienced the worship of the East through his visits to Ukrainian Uniat monasteries. The Uniat Churches, although united with Rome, had been allowed to preserve their own rites in the vernacular (this in itself a challenge to the universal Latin Mass) and provided a means of contact with the East. In setting up a dual-rite monastic house (now at Chevetogne) Beauduin brought the experience of Eastern worship to Belgium and the West and provided personal contact between individual priests and monks which would have further extended the influence. As already noted in Chapter 4, the impact of Beauduin's work was considerable. Through the Malines conversations his thoughts extended into the Anglican Church, providing a further influence upon the growth of the Parish Communion Movement and openness to the Liturgical Movement in general.

A second and entirely separate route of influence was to develop in South India where the Syrian Orthodox liturgy of St James provided a significant input into the new CSI rite (see Chapter 6). From this were acquired the epiclesis and also the passing of the Peace between the people, together with the acclamations in the eucharistic prayer. Through this rather circuitous route these Eastern features have found their way not only into the new Anglican and Methodist orders but also into the new Roman rite. The effects of the Eastern Churches continue to be felt. In particular, the issue of infant communion is under consideration in some of the Anglican provinces and may eventually prove a further primitive and Eastern insight to be adopted.

The picture painted so far may appear to indicate a single one-way influence of the East upon the West in the Liturgical Movement. It must be acknowledged, however, that the process has been one of looking back rather than simply looking East. Many of the Eastern practices have been adopted because they were recognized as early Church forms preserved by Orthodoxy. More recent Orthodox development such as the icon screen and the very limited active participation of the laity in worship have not been appropriated. It is perhaps significant that no Western Church has adopted an Eastern rite in its totality. (The so-called Common Eucharistic Prayer, popular in North America, which is virtually the same as Eucharistic Prayer 4 of the revised Roman rite, is based on the anaphora of St Basil and is perhaps the most significant example of direct textual borrowing. Litanies based on Eastern models have also been borrowed.)

The Liturgical Movement has also developed emphases lacking in the East. The formal, mystical style of the East has not always competed well against the desire for brevity and informality. The relationship between mission and worship is less explicit in Orthodoxy though it is undoubtedly true that the decisive factor in the conversion of many to Orthodoxy has been experience of the liturgy. (The Orthodox missionary James Stamoolis quotes with approval the observation that, 'the liturgy is the strongest appeal of the Church'.)[1] Furthermore, whereas the East has been concerned to *preserve* ancient traditions, the modern Liturgical Movement has a fresh desire to see ongoing modification. There are differences too, over liturgical language. As we shall discuss in Chapter 14, in many parts of the Western Church there is now a need to maintain comprehensibility and to ensure the expression of new insights. In the Eastern Churches changing the archaic language forms is particularly difficult. Not only is the sense of tradition very strong, but the forms are known by heart by worshippers who often have a low level of literacy and for whom the reading of a text from a book would be totally alien. In addition, some Orthodox writers would maintain that the traditional language of worship 'was *never* a "contemporary" or "spoken" language', but was 'consciously artificial', even though it was never intentionally obscure or unintelligible.[2]

Another point of divergence is the impact of the Charismatic Movement (see Chapter 11) which has challenged much of the Western Church to allow new life into its structures, but has had little or no impact on the East.

Yet, despite the apparent lack of change in the Eastern Churches, the assessment that, 'the Orthodox Churches have so far experienced nothing resembling the so-called

[1] Stamoolis, *Orthodox Mission Theology*, p. 100.
[2] Mother Mary and Ware, *The Festal Menaion*, p. 14.

Liturgical Movement which has so affected contemporary worship in the Western Churches',[3] is perhaps too sweeping. The lack of freedom imposed by living under Islamic or Communist domination has made reform difficult but it would be wrong to assume that the Eastern Churches are not alive to many of the concerns of the Liturgical Movement. As long ago as the eighteenth century, for example, Archbishop Makarios Notaras of Corinth published a handbook on the many benefits of frequent communion, and it was an important theme in the writings of the influential Athonite monk Nicodemos the Hagiorite (*c.* 1749–1809) who drew attention to the importance the early Fathers attached to it. In Russia, Father John of Kronstadt, whose remarkable ministry at the naval base near St Petersburg covered most of the second half of the nineteenth century, also taught the necessity of frequent communion, and, since his congregations were too large for him to hear individual confessions on each occasion, instituted a form of public confession, with worshippers confessing their sins to one another. He also replaced the large icon screen with the more primitive low wall, thus enabling greater visibility and active participation.[4] In the months following the fall of the Tsar and the Bolshevik Revolution, bold reforms – including a new Calendar, simplification of the services and the use of modern language – were proposed in the Russian Orthodox Church. Atheistic persecution prevented the implementation of any reforms and it remains to be seen whether following the collapse of the Soviet Union the Russian Orthodox Church will again address the possibility of liturgical reform.

Elsewhere among the Eastern Churches liturgical renewal is being increasingly advocated and cautiously implemented in places. In some churches in Greece, for example,

[3] Wybrew, *Orthodox Liturgy*, p. 174.

[4] Grisbrooke, *Spiritual Counsels*, p. xxiii.

prayers usually said silently by the celebrant are now said aloud and the doors of the iconostasis are left open during the liturgy. The influential Orthodox theologian Alexander Schmemann has written extensively on liturgical theology, seeking to demonstrate the unity of doctrine, worship and pastoral ministrations. Schmemann believes that the Orthodox Church is in a 'profound liturgical crisis'.[5] This, he maintains, is due not simply to defects in contemporary liturgical practice, but to the degeneration of the Church into a 'cultic society' with a consequent loss of wider vision. Other writers have made the same point. Emilianos Timiades, for example, speaks of the need for 'a rethinking of our worship in relation to man's challenge and his new cultural setting', and sees the need to 'proceed to adaptations of the liturgy and to reshape the structure of worship.[6] Such calls have been taken up officially at various pan-Orthodox conferences, but so far no widespread revision has been attempted among the Byzantine family of Churches.

Within the Oriental Orthodox Churches a modest attempt at revision was made in the nineteenth century by a section of the Syrian Orthodox Church in India. The advent of the Anglican Church Missionary Society in 1816 led to a call by some Indian Orthodox priests for the removal of what were seen to be doctrinal aberrations in their traditional Syrian rites. Features such as the invocation of saints and prayers for the departed were removed, together with a slight simplification of ceremonial. The vernacular Malayalam was substituted for Syriac. The attempted reform became associated with other factors, notably the independence of the Indian Church from the Syrian Orthodox Church in the Middle East, and eventually a split ensued. The various rites of the Mar Thoma Syrian

[5] Alexander Schmemann, *An Introduction to Liturgical Theology*, London, Faith Press, 1966, p. 21.

[6] 'The Renewal of Orthodox Worship', p. 95.

Church – as the followers of the reforming bishops eventually became – remain substantially Orthodox, though there still exists a lack (such as that identified by Schmemann among the Byzantines) of active appreciation of the liturgy as a source of doctrine and mission.

Mention should also be made of the Maronite Church in Lebanon which has, in the last two decades, revised its ancient Syriac services, streamlining them, and translating them into modern Arabic, or, for the American Maronite community, English. The links with the Roman Catholic Church and this Uniat Church have been a catalyst.

In conclusion, the debt of the Western Churches to the East in providing the impetus for liturgical change has been considerable. As the Western Church becomes a minority in its own society (as many of the Eastern Churches are in theirs) it is possible that parallels between the two sides of Christendom will increase. However, the Liturgical Movement has arguably drawn on what the East has preserved, rather than what it is doing today. As the East continues to find change difficult, the pace of development in the West may ultimately mean that the major influence of East upon West is now past.

Selected Reading

Alexander Mar Thoma, *The Mar Thoma Church: Heritage and Mission*, Kottayam, 2nd edn., 1986.

W. Jardine Grisbrooke, *The Spiritual Counsels of Father John of Kronstadt*, London, James Clarke & Co., 1967.

Juhanon Mar Thoma, *Christianity in India and a Brief History of the Mar Thoma Syrian Church*, Madras, 1968.

F. Kanichikattil, *To Restore or to Reform*, Bangalore, Dharmasam Publications, 1992.

G. Mathew (ed.), *A Study on the Malankara Mar Thoma Church Liturgy*, Manganam, Kottayam, 1993.

Mother Mary and T. Ware, *The Festal Menaion*, London, Faber & Faber, 1984.

A. Schmemann, 'The Liturgical Problem', in *St Vladimir's Theological Quarterly*, 8 (1964), pp. 164–85.

H-J. Schulz, *The Byzantine Liturgy*, ET New York, Pueblo Press, 1986.

Bryan D. Spinks, *Western Use and Abuse of Eastern Liturgical Traditions*, Centre for Indian and Inter-religious Studies, Rome, 1992.

J. J. Stamoolis, *Eastern Orthodox Mission Theology Today*, Maryknoll, New York, Orbis Books, 1986.

R. Taft, *The Byzantine Rite: A Short History*, Collegeville, Liturgical Press, 1993.

E. Timiades, 'The Renewal of Orthodox Worship', in *Studia Liturgica*, 6, 1969, pp. 95–116.

H. Wybrew, *The Orthodox Liturgy*, London, SPCK, 1989.

11

The Impact of the Charismatic Movement

For hundreds of thousands – perhaps millions – of Christians throughout the world the last few decades of the twentieth century have brought a totally new experience of worship of unimagined intensity. This has not at first glance, however, had anything to do with the Liturgical Movement, but with a wave of revival and renewal in the Holy Spirit which has swept through many of the mainline Churches – the Charismatic Movement. The movement has usually been associated with a powerful experience in the life of the individuals concerned, often accompanied by speaking in tongues and other 'gifts' (such as healing and prophecy) such as are described in the New Testament. There is a sense of immediacy in the Charismatic Movement which would initially seem at odds with the rediscovery of tradition which has been such a prominent feature of the Liturgical Movement. In fact, however, the relationship between them is complex and bears more detailed examination.

The development of the Charismatic Movement

As with all movements, the beginning of the modern Charismatic Movement is difficult to identify precisely. The re-examination of church history which the movement has prompted has confirmed the existence down the centuries in different parts of the Church of phenomena – tongues, healing, prophecy, visions – which are features both of the New Testament and of the recent revival. There have been disputes as to whether particular manifestations are in fact the same thing at different periods, but in general the persistence of what might be described as 'supernatural' experiences in the life of the Church is vindicated.

Within the twentieth century two waves or phases of the Charismatic Movement might be discerned. The first, originating in the early years of the century, led to the proliferation of Pentecostal denominations in many parts of the world. The second phase, dating from around 1950, saw the acceptance of 'Pentecostalist' experience and insights into many existing Churches, though some loss of membership to newly founded groupings has also occurred.

A traditional starting date for the modern Charismatic Movement is 9 April 1906 when 'fire came down' at a prayer meeting held in Bonnie Brae Street, Los Angeles, conducted by the black preacher W. J. Seymour. Worshippers experienced a 'baptism in the Spirit' and spoke in tongues. Large numbers of people became caught up in the experience which eventually moved its base to Azusa Street Mission which is 'regarded by the Pentecostalist as the place of origin of the worldwide Pentecostal movement'.[1] Many of those involved in the early years had a background in the various Holiness Churches, and the importance of this strand of spirituality and worship – stretching back to the eighteenth century and associated with John Wesley – should not be underestimated. Revivals which included some Pentecostalist features in places like Wales and Germany had pre-dated the events of Azusa Street.

The experience of Pentecostal worship and its stress on tongues and other 'charismata' was strongly at odds with the ethos and liturgical practice of most Roman Catholic, Anglican and Protestant worship at the beginning of the twentieth century. Any worshippers within these Churches who became involved in the revival were

[1] Hollenweger, *Pentecostals*, p. 22.

usually required to leave and join 'Pentecostalist' Churches. The movement spread rapidly in North and South America, but made less headway in Europe. Following the Second World War two important developments tookplace. First, Pentecostalism as a distinct expression of the Christian faith in a sense 'came of age'. Many congregations were now several decades old and had taken on a form which complemented rather than threatened the mainline Churches. In the 1950s the South African David du Plessis, as General Secretary of the World Pentecostal Conferences, worked hard at building links with traditional Churches (including the Roman Catholic Church) and with ecumenical bodies such as the WCC. His openness did much to encourage a more positive attitude towards Pentecostalism and its insights among those outside the movement. The highly successful book, *The Cross and the Switchblade*, about Pentecostal pastor David Wilkerson's work with street gangs and drug addicts in New York, caught the imagination of many in the post-war youth culture and did much to commend a Spirit-filled life to a younger generation.

Second, increasing ecumenical openness brought a rapid cross-fertilization through books and personal contacts. In the same year that a student was asked to leave one of the Church of England's theological colleges for initiating a Pentecostal prayer group, the Anglo-Catholic priest Dennis Bennett announced to his parishioners in Van Nuys, California, that he and a number of people in the parish had received 'the fullness of the Holy Spirit'. Bennett subsequently published his story (*Nine o'Clock in the Morning*, London, Fountain Trust, 1970) and remained convinced that an experience of the Holy Spirit of this nature was wholly compatible with being a sacramentally orientated episcopalian. In 1962, two years after Bennett's experience, the Rev Michael Harper, curate of the prestigious Evangelical Anglican Church of All Souls, Langham Place, in London, had an experience of the Holy Spirit while preparing a study on Ephesians. Harper was invited to speak on the Holy Spirit at many churches and in July 1964 became the first Director of the Fountain Trust, the aim of which was to promote charismatic renewal. (Interestingly, Harper linked up with Du Plessis at this time.) The Fountain Trust through its staff and publications was to play an important role in stimulating spiritual revival, especially in Britain, and voluntarily came to an end in 1980 largely because it believed that the renewal movement was so firmly established in the parishes and structures of the Church (especially the theological colleges) that a specific agency or organ was no longer needed.

The language and ultimately the experience of the Charismatic Movement penetrated the Roman Catholic Church also. At Pentecost 1959 Pope John XXIII announced the summoning of the Second Vatican Council with the words, 'All the bishops of the Church . . . are to be gathered at a new Pentecost'. The expectation of the work of the Spirit is further illustrated by the Pope's prayer: 'Holy Spirit, sent by the Father in the name of Jesus, be present in the Church and lead it continually. We beseech you to pour out the fullness of your gifts on this Ecumenical Council. Renew your wonders in our day. Give us a new Pentecost.' Many would see the answer to the Pope's prayer not simply in the reforms initiated by the Council itself, but in the widespread penetration of the Roman Catholic Church by the Charismatic Movement. Groups of Catholics worshipping informally together alongside the normal parochial worship sprang up in many places. In time something of the new spirit of worship was to become part of regular worship. This is particularly true of the hymns and choruses that the Charismatic Movement inspired. The high point of the Roman Catholic Charismatic Movement came at Pentecost 1975 when ten thousand Catholics from sixty-three countries met for the third International Congress of

Catholic Renewal in Rome. Cardinal Suenens presided at the eucharist at St Peter's with twelve bishops and seven hundred and fifty priests concelebrating. There was singing in tongues and prophecy confirmed by long applause from the congregation.

While not denying the 'Pentecostalist' input into the Charismatic Movement, Cardinal Suenens has increasingly testified to his own and the movement's indebtedness to two of the Liturgical Movement's roots:

> I first realized the importance of the Holy Spirit when I met Dom Lambert Beauduin in Rome in the early twenties. He shared with contagious enthusiasm about the Holy Spirit and Trinitarian theology. I listened intently. We were then going through a kind of 'deist' phase in which the Holy Spirit disappeared in God and had no personal reality. Dom Lambert reacted against this impoverishment. For me it was like a flash of light . . . We must never forget that Renewal is also deeply indebted to the Eastern traditions which have always been alive to the role of the Holy Spirit, as the Council Fathers of the Eastern Churches constantly stressed during Vatican II.

In the 1970s and 1980s the Charismatic Movement entered what might be termed a global phase. Roman Catholics began to pioneer renewal in South America. In the Anglican Communion charismatic bishops met together at Canterbury prior to the 1978 Lambeth Conference. Subsequently there was set up the network SOMA (Sharing of Ministries Abroad) which encouraged renewal and exchange throughout the Communion. More recently the Ecumenical International Charismatic Consultation on World Evangelization has brought together those working for renewal in the different Churches. New spurts of advance continue to take place, often associated with particular individuals (such as John Wimber) or phenomena (for example, the 'Toronto blessing'), but in the main the Charismatic Movement's spread has become more 'low key', with the effect of leavening the lump.

Characteristics of the Charismatic Movement

With its emphasis on the presence and reality of God, charismatic worship is in part at least a reaction against the aridity of both the personal lives of individual Christians and the dryness of the public worship of many congregations. The movement thus constitutes a warning that 'no organization, no structuring, no texts, no music and no minister will be of any use if they do not actually bring people into touch with God'. For many Christians – including those whose experience of corporate worship had been reshaped by the Liturgical Movement – there was a missing experience, and inner thirst that only an experience of God himself can satisfy.

An important characteristic of the Charismatic Movement has been its predominantly lay character. 'Ordinary' Christians have been 'released' into exercising gifts in areas of ministry such as healing, evangelism, teaching and preaching which had hitherto been the preserve of the ordained. 'Every member ministry' became an important theme: all had been given gifts by the Holy Spirit to be used in the building up the People of God and extending his Kingdom. The dominant sense of 'release' – including forgiveness of sin – has led to a more positive appreciation of the body and of the natural world. This is reflected in the use of the body in worship through dance and uplifted hands, and through the use of colour and beauty (seen, for example, in the creation of banners) in Churches which traditionally had not had such an 'incarnational' emphasis. Informality and an atmosphere of joy are also typical.

A further important feature of the Charismatic Movement has been the way in which it has helped to erode denominational boundaries. Catholics and Protestants, for example, have been forced to take each other seriously as fellow Christians in the light of a common experience of the Holy Spirit. Widely differing Churches are experiencing an increase in missionary zeal, reflected in part by the designation of the 1990s as the Decade of Evangelism/ Evangelization by the Anglican Communion, Roman Catholic Church and others.

The Charismatic Movement has however had its negative features. There have been internal squabbles and divisions when insensitive or hasty handling of the renewal has led to its being rejected by some Churches and congregations. Individuals have felt isolated in their Churches and have joined the networks of 'House Churches' which have experienced rapid growth in many places. These too have had their difficulties: dominant personalities, unbalanced teaching and an excessively authoritarian style have characterized some. In places the House Churches are already beginning to experience the problems of the second generation – how to keep the flames of renewal alight with the passing of time. Sometimes there has been a misuse of gifts and excesses that have taken advantage of naïve and vulnerable individuals and groups.

On balance, however, the Charismatic Movement has brought new life and confidence to Churches which were flagging in the face of Western secularism. The movement has arguably provided a new framework for discussing old issues, such as the efficacy of the sacraments and the validity of ministries. Its influence extends far beyond those congregations which would call themselves 'charismatic'.

The relationship between the Charismatic Movement and the Liturgical Movement

It is undoubtedly the case that the Charismatic Movement and the Liturgical Movement are related; the question is *how* they are related. Did one feed off the other? Are they parallel or do they diverge? Do they need each other? There are a significant number of similarities which help to begin to answer such questions.

Both movements have urged an interest in the early Church: the Liturgical Movement as a source of liturgical shape, the Charismatic Movement as a quarry for pneumatological precedent, thinking and experience. Both have stressed community and participation: the Liturgical Movement drawing on Catholic and Eastern structures, and the Charismatic Movement in a recognition of the renewed vitality and oneness that the Holy Spirit gives within and between individuals and Churches. The list could be extended to include their similar concerns for the reinstatement of the Bible in liturgy and life, the centrality of the eucharist, informality and liturgical space, and the need for worship to be accessible to the individual worshipper – in the vernacular and not encrusted with dry ritual.

Despite such similarities, the movements are clearly not the same. The essential heart of the Charismatic Movement is pneumatology. This pneumatology is preached, proclaimed and practised. It is exhibited psychologically in a new desire to worship and sociologically in a new desire to associate in worship with other Christians. Whilst the Liturgical Movement had undoubtedly had a pneumatological element (seen, for example in the widespread restoration of an epiclesis in Western rites), it has not stressed the 'personal epiclesis' which the Charismatic Movement has brought to many. There is little evidence that the Liturgical Movement contained in itself the seeds of Spirit-centred revival prior to its exposure to some of the influences described earlier in this chapter. The work of Beauduin, de Candole, Hebert and Frere was foundational in creating a spirit of change, but they did not preach 'baptism in the Spirit'. Conversely, it is easy to see that the preaching of Anglican and Roman Catholic charismatics would have found no ready ears if the ground had not already been prepared. In this respect the Liturgical Movement undoubtedly provided the 'seedbed' (to use Buchanan's word) for charismatic renewal. The Liturgical Movement did not give birth to the Charismatic Movement, but it provided an incubator for its early development. The setting for charismatic renewal was internal to the Liturgical Movement, but the impetus for experience and expression of charismata came from outside. Since the beginning of the century the Liturgical Movement had been unconsciously preparing the way for the expression of the Charismatic Movement within the traditional Churches. In the first half of the century the ecclesiastical wineskins were too inflexible to have contained the new wine of charismatic renewal. In the second half of the century the Liturgical Movement had rendered them sufficiently supple to contain the effervescent new life without too much spillage.

The future relationship of the two movements is hard to predict. The Charismatic Movement is still spreading into new congregations, but perhaps more slowly and less dramatically than before. Frequently in a parish it has been the 'renewed' members who have provided the impetus to initiate change in line with the insights of the Liturgical Movement. There is currently what might be described as a symbiotic relationship. Its future course is difficult to predict.

Selected Reading

C. O. Buchanan, *Encountering Charismatic Worship*, Bramcote, Grove Books, 1977.

Church of England Report, *The Charismatic Movement in the Church of England*, London, CIO, 1981.

J. D. G. Dunn, *Baptism in the Holy Spirit*, London, SCM, 1970.

J. Gunstone, 'The Spirit's Freedom in the Spirit's Framework', in K. Stevenson, *Liturgy Reshaped*, London, SPCK, 1982.

M. Harper, *As at the Beginning*, London, Hodder, 1965.

W. J. Hollenweger, *The Pentecostals*, London, SCM, 1972.

— article 'Pentecostal Worship', in J. G. Davies (ed.), *A New Dictionary of Liturgy and Worship*, London, SCM, 1986.

G. Kendrick, *Worship*, Eastbourne, Kingsway, 1984.

K. McDonnell, *Presence, Power, Praise*, 3 vols., Collegeville, Liturgical Press, 1980.

M. Marshall, *Renewal in Worship*, London, Marshall Morgan & Scott, 1982.

L. Newbigin, *The Household of God*, London, SCM, 1953.

J. Steven, *Worship in the Restoration Movement*, Bramcote, Grove Books, 1989.

12

Behind the Consensus on the Eucharist

A comparison of the majority of new eucharistic liturgies reveals that the Liturgical Movement has left behind a remarkable degree of consensus on the structure and content of the eucharistic liturgy. The 1963 WCC Montreal Conference stated:

> Orders of Holy Communion usually include the following elements:
>
> a) A Service of the Word, containing:
>   i. the reading and preaching of the Word.
>   ii. intercession for the whole church and the world.
>
> b) A Service of the Sacrament, having a shape determined by the actions of our Lord at the Last Supper:
>   i. taking bread and wine to be used by God in this service.
>   ii. blessing God for creation and redemption and invoking the Holy Spirit, or referring in some other way to the Holy Spirit, reciting the Words of Institution, whether before or within or after the prayer of thanksgiving, saying the Lord's Prayer.
>   iii. breaking the bread.
>   iv. giving the bread and the wine.
>
> This list of liturgical items is not meant to exclude reference during the service to many other important theological themes such as the expression of contrition, the declaration of forgiveness of sins, the affirmation of faith in creedal form, the celebration of the communion of saints, the announcement of the Lord's Coming and the self-dedication of the faithful to God.[1]

[1] *Studia Liturgica*, 2 (1963), pp. 243–55, p. 248.

A very similar structural consensus was outlined by the JLG *Initiation and Eucharist* (1972). The amount of cross-fertilization that has taken place between the Churches has blurred the distinction between their rites. We find a distinct Liturgy of the Word and Liturgy of the Sacrament. The first has an entrance rite, Old Testament, New Testament and Gospel lections, sermon and intercessions. The second contains the placing of the elements on the table, the eucharistic prayer, usually a fraction, the act of communion, and a short post-communion rite with blessing and dismissal. In one sense, to have read one new rite is to have read them all. There is indeed a remarkable consensus. It is useful, however, to look behind this consensus.

Different paths

In the Roman Catholic rite the path followed was one of streamlining and restoration. The programme was outlined in the Constitution on the Sacred Liturgy (CSL) 50–56, and may be summarized as follows:

1. The Ordinary of the Mass was to be revised to reveal more clearly the real function of each part.
2. The rites were to be simplified; doublets and additions of little value were to be omitted.
3. A greater and more varied use of Scripture was enjoined, and the lections spread over a number of years.
4. The homily is a real part of the liturgy, and must not be omitted on Sundays and holy days of obligation.
5. The common prayers or intercessions were to be restored.

These few points were in fact sufficient to alter the structure of the Tridentine Mass.

In the Anglican Church, followed to some degree by Methodists and the Reformed Churches, the consensus has been reached by radical reshaping. The Anglican revisions started from the *Book of Common Prayer* and its various adaptations in the Anglican Communion. Revision has been concerned with altering the structure of the 1637 and 1662 shapes to reach the consensus. The 1958 Lambeth Conference was an important landmark, and it recommended the following structure:

At the antecommunion (Liturgy of the Word):

1. An Old Testament lesson should be used.
2. Psalmody be used between the readings.
3. The creed to follow the sermon.
4. The *Gloria in excelsis* to come at the beginning of the service.
5. The use of a litany-form of intercession.

At the communion:

1. The offertory to be more closely connected with the prayer of consecration.
2. The events for which thanksgiving is made in the consecration prayer are not to be confined to Calvary but include thanksgiving for all the principal 'mighty works of God'.

The subcommittee which reported to the Lambeth Conference proposed that a committee should be appointed whose task it would be to prepare an outline of the structure of the Holy Communion service for the Anglican Communion, for there was a danger that each province would set out in a different direction. The outcome was a document called 'The Structure and Contents of the Eucharistic Liturgy' (1965), which came to be known as the Pan-Anglican document (see Chapter 8). It noted five phases in the celebration of the full eucharist:

1. The Preparation.
2. The Service of the Word of God.
3. The Great Intercession.
4. The Service of the Lord's Supper.
5. The Dismissal.

A second Pan-Anglican document appeared in 1968, identifying eight elements in the celebration. The actual interplay between these documents and certain influential experimental revisions is outlined in the collections edited by Colin Buchanan. These documents, together with the influence of Gregory Dix's four action shape (see Chapter 5 and below) resulted in radical reshaping, including the rewriting of the so-called prayer of consecration.

English Methodist and URC, and Church of Scotland revision was in the hands of smaller groups. Significant recovery of a Catholic pattern of eucharistic liturgy had already been achieved in the Church of Scotland *Book of Common Order* 1940, and that of 1979 entailed modernizing and tidying up. Although not slavishly following the Anglican revisions in England, the English Methodist and URC liturgies reshaped their respective patterns of eucharist to arrive at a similar consensus.

The act of penitence: position and tone

In the Roman rite, the Tridentine High Mass had no public confession. There was a confession for clergy and servers – the old *Confiteor* – and through the Dialogue Mass it had been recited by priest and congregation. Historically, however, it was a private devotion of the priest, and not part of the Mass, though it took on a prominent position at Low Mass, and its popularity here was one reason for its inclusion in the new rite. The penitential rite of the new Mass comes at the beginning, and has three alternatives, taking two forms: either a form of the old *Confiteor* said by all, followed by absolution, or alternative versicles and responses, the second of which is based around the *Kyries*. (The *Kyries* may still be used if either of the first two alternatives are used.) The absolution (always the same form) is very short, and is collective: 'have mercy on us'.

The 1662 *Book of Common Prayer* (BCP) had a confession, absolution and comfortable words, all ultimately deriving from the Order of Hermann von Wied of Cologne in 1543, placed after the 'Church Militant' and before the *Sursum corda*. In the new revisions in the Church of England, beginning with Series 1, the confession was resituated before the offertory. It maintained this position, though various alternative forms were allowed. In the ASB the penitential section could come at the beginning before the *Kyries* and *Gloria*. The literary form of the confession has a disgraceful history. A new form written by David Frost was rejected for a very uninspiring form composed very hastily. David Frost wrote:

> But some time after tea on that November afternoon (10 November 1971) when some of the more interested members had gone home, believing that the Chairman would not permit resumed discussion on the service, Synod was overtaken by a fit of winter madness. The Bishops sat bewildered, and made only a single last-minute intervention. It was, as one respected diocesan later put it, 'as if the party of schoolboys had suddenly discovered that it was permitted to throw stones at the headmaster'. Within a quarter of an hour, the Commission's Confession was thrown out, to be replaced by the notorious 'Cockin Confession', drafted, it was later alleged, on the back of an envelope.[2]

The absolution when given by a priest retains the ministerial form 'have mercy on you', as does the American BCP 1979.

The English Methodist 1936 communion order had the same rearrangement as the 1662 BCP. The 1975 rite has the confession at the beginning, and follows the earlier Anglican Series 3 formula. It is followed by a declaration of forgiveness, similar to that of the JLG Daily Office, 1969: 'Christ Jesus came into the world to save sinners. Hear then the Word of Grace. Your sins are forgiven.'

The URC 1980 and 1989 books place the confession at the beginning, but this is the position it has normally had in the

[2] David L. Frost, *The Language of Series 3*, Grove Booklet on Ministry and Worship 12, Bramcote, 1973, p. 18. The main author of this text was alleged to be Canon Cockin, hence the term 'Cockin Confession'.

Calvinist tradition. The 1989 book provides three forms of confession (two in responsory form) and two forms of 'Assurance of Pardon', only slightly different from the 1980 forms. The 'Assurance of Pardon' is couched in indirect terms:

> In repentence and in faith receive the promise of grace and the assurance of pardon:
>
> Here are words you may trust, words that merit full acceptance: 'Christ Jesus came into the world to save sinners.'
>
> To all who turn to him he says: 'Your sins are forgiven.' He also says: 'Follow me.'
>
> or,
>
> God so loved the world that he gave his only Son, that everyone who has faith in him may not perish but have eternal life.
>
> To all who repent and believe, we declare in the name of the Father, the Son, and the Holy Spirit: God grants you the forgiveness of your sins.

The American BCP 1979 and the Lutheran *Book of Worship* 1978 both provide the act of confession and absolution before the actual eucharistic liturgy. It can be used separately or as a preparation for the eucharist.

Perhaps three theological points are worth considering.

1. Absolution versus assurance of pardon. Ultimately this distinction must surely be only a literary difference. Whether one uses scriptural quotations with the assertion that God forgives, or whether the minister, speaking for the Church, declares sins are forgiven, both are entirely dependent upon the gospel message of Jesus, and both derive their authority solely from him. Oddly, the 1984 Norwegian Lutheran rite has a confession at the beginning, followed by the *Kyries*, but no declaration of pardon.

2. The place of the Act of Penitence. Some have felt that it should come at the beginning because entering into the presence of God makes us aware of the contrast

between our sinfulness and God's holiness. Most new rites therefore place penitence at the beginning. Some Anglican rites place it further on, after the intercessions. The argument is that in the gospels repentence comes after the proclamation of the good news. However, if this is accepted, then the logical place would be after the sermon and before the Creed.

3. In the light of the gospel parables, perhaps the order confession-absolution is odd. Jeremias argued that whereas in Judaism forgiveness followed repentence and restitution, Jesus offended Jewish piety by reversing the sequence. E. P. Sanders has gone even further, suggesting that the later repentance is a later gloss, and that Jesus offered forgiveness simply by association with himself, without the need for repentance! One wonders whether God's prior forgiveness needs to be articulated in the declaration of pardon, such as by putting the URC form into the past tense – God has already granted the forgiveness of your sins.

The lections and lectionaries

At a superficial level the arrangement of the lections in most modern eucharistic liturgies is the same: an Old Testament lesson has been restored; there is provision for psalmody between the Epistle and the Gospel; and after the reading of the Gospel comes the homily or sermon. Furthermore, the lectionary is not repeated every year. It is either triennial or biennial. However, in reality in England at least there are two distinct lectionary systems in use, based on different ideas about the liturgical lections:

1. The Roman Catholic triennial lectionary.

2. The JLG biennial lectionary, which forms the basic lectionary of the Church of England, Church of Scotland, Methodist and URC lections.

The basis of the Roman Catholic revision of the eucharistic lections was set out in articles 24, 35 and 51 of CSL. The Consilium set to work in 1964, with both Germany and France offering plans for reform.[3] Gaston Fontaine of Canada made a systematic collection of biblical passages used in various rites, ancient and modern. Thirty-one Bible scholars were given the task of selecting from the various books passages which were thought suitable for reading in church. In fact, three distinct lectionaries were devised: Sundays; weekdays; and Saints' days. A triennial lectionary was chosen, with years designated A, B and C. C is read in the years divisible by three – so, for example, 1992 was year C. In year A the Gospel lections are mainly from St Matthew; year B, St Mark and St John; and year C, St Luke. John is also read in Lent and at Eastertide. Some important festivals have the same readings, whatever the year, such as Easter and Pentecost. Generally there is an Old Testament lesson, though Acts is sometimes substituted, and sometimes Revelation replaces an Epistle. Acts and Revelation are used throughout Eastertide.

In working out this lectionary there were two opposing theories; should the readings be semi-continuous or thematic? The solution was a compromise. The Old Testament lesson is usually connected with the Gospel, though at festivals all the readings have a similar theme. Quite often the Epistle is independent, and at some seasons is read as a semi-continuous reading. The Gradual psalm was chosen according to whether it is quoted in one of the lections, has a literary relationship with the lections, or has been traditionally used at a particular season.

There is a tension, therefore, between a scholarly approach which allows the different books to speak for themselves – so, for example, the integrity of each evangelist is acknowledged – and a typological approach which seems demanded

[3] Bugnini, *The Reform of the Liturgy 1948–1975*, Collegeville, Liturgical Press, 1990, pp. 406ff.

by the guidelines for the homily. It is all too easy to try to link the lections and preach a model patristic-style homily, which ignores 150 years of critical scholarship.

In America the new Roman lectionary was adapted first by the United Presbyterian Church, and subsequently by the Episcopal and Lutheran Churches. Other North American Churches followed suit, with the result that the Consultation on Common Texts, an ecumenical body, published the *Common Lectionary* in the hope that a new ecumenical lectionary could be used by all major denominations in North America. These hopes are at present unfulfilled, since Rome did not give permission for the Roman Catholics to use the *Common Lectionary*, and the Episcopalian Church has had second thoughts about its use. However, the Consultation on Common Texts published *The Revised Common Lectionary* 1992, hoping that this would commend itself to the various interested Churches.

The criticisms levelled at the Roman lectionary are even more acute with regard to the JLG lectionary which underlies the lectionaries of most of the Churches of the United Kingdom. The origin of this lectionary can be traced to three separate factors:

1. The work of the Presbyterian scholar, Allan McArthur, *The Christian Year and Lectionary Reform* (1958), which advocated a lectionary based on a calendar concerned with the life of Christ.
2. The Church of South India lectionary which re-arranged the Sundays of the Christian Year and added an Old Testament lesson to the eucharist.
3. The popularity in the 1950s of what was termed 'biblical theology'.

A possible unifying agent of these factors was Bishop Henry de Candole (see Chapter 5). As President of Parish and People he had urged the necessity of headings to explain lections, and he espoused the biblical theology school of thought. As a member of both the Church of England

Liturgical Commission and the JLG, he together with the Baptist scholar, Neville Clark, produced the 1965 JLG *Calendar and Lectionary*, though it is clear that the Methodist liturgist, Raymond George, was also a strong advocate. De Candole's thinking can already be seen in articles in *Theology* in 1960, 'Can we Rationalize the Christian Year?' and 1962, 'Sundays after Trinity', and in *Parish and People* 36, 1963, 'Old Testament Lections: An Indian Initiative'. The JLG openly advocated a thematic lectionary based upon the Christian Year. The particular Sunday determines the theme, which in turn determines the lections.

Although this is an excellent teaching lectionary, it has considerable weaknesses. To begin with, any lectionary which ties itself too closely to a particular school of biblical scholarship risks becoming dated, and 'biblical theology' of the 1950s is certainly dated. Furthermore, by wedding the lections so closely to a thematic calendar, the Church already determines what the message of Scripture will be. Of course, all lectionaries are selective, but here Scripture hardly dictates its own terms. Furthermore, the thematic approach does not respect the integrity of each biblical writer. Thus, for example, the synoptic gospels are picked and harmonized to the point of reducing them to pulp, and the lesson of redaction criticism that each has its own message is ignored. Furthermore, in the original JLG lectionary, there were many omissions of passages concerned with the judgement of God, suggesting that this was a product of the euphoria of the 1960s.

In 1990 the JLG published a Four Year lectionary, designed to meet some of the criticisms made against its original lectionary. The claim is made that the themes have been adandoned and a year given to each gospel. However, it is still bound to the JLG calendar, which has been abandoned in recent draft material in the Church of England, and the 1994 Church of Scotland *Book of Common Order* has adopted the *Revised Common Lectionary*. It has, however, been included in the latest Baptist liturgy, *Patterns and Prayers for*

Christian Worship. The previous JLG has been called the thematic lectionary in contrast to the redactionist lectionary of Rome; this recent lectionary has been dubbed by some the 'Fundamentalist Lectionary' because it appears to make no distinction between the suitability of certain traditional gospel material at certain seasons from one gospel in preference to the others.

The general intercessions

An important part of Christian worship is intercession, and Justin Martyr notes that this was part of the eucharistic liturgy in the second century. Whether or not the Jewish Eighteen Benedictions were the origin of these intercessions is highly debatable; but what is less debatable is the fact that 1 Tim. 2:1–7 became a starting point for the pattern of Christian intercession. In the Roman rite, other than in the Canon of the Mass, intercessions had disappeared. It used to be argued that the oldest forms of Roman intercession were those found in the Solemn Prayers for Good Friday. As a regular Sunday feature, they were last referred to by Pope Felix III (483–92) and were thought to have been replaced by Pope Gelasius with a litany after the Greek style, placed at the beginning of the rite. Under Pope Gregory I the litany disappeared leaving only the *Kyries*.

More recent scholarship has questioned this simple story. G. G. Willis has shown that the collects of the Solemn Prayers of Good Friday are not as ancient as the biddings.[4] It would seem that the earliest liturgical form of intercessions in the Roman rite (third century) was biddings for certain things and people, followed by private prayer. Paul de Clerck noted that in the fifth century there appeared litanies which were more or less simply translations from the Eastern rites.[5]

[4] G. G. Willis, *Essays in Early Roman Liturgy*, 1964.

[5] Paul de Clerck, *La Prière Universelle dans les liturgies latines anciennes*, 1977.

He identified two phases: simple translations, and then, towards the end of the fifth century, litanies composed in the Latin idiom. These co-existed with the earlier type found in the Solemn Prayers, and these litanies existed before the time of Pope Gelasius. The earlier type fell into disuse simply because the litany form was more popular. De Clerck challenges the view that the *Kyries* are the remnant of a litany, suggesting that they were a deliberate chant introduced into the rite.

Whatever the historical truth, the Bidding Prayers of the new Roman rite represents a restoration of an element which had disappeared. In 1965 ICEL published some suggestions for the form the biddings might take. The ultimate form, which is the freest part of the Roman rite, was simply a heading 'the Prayer of the Faithful' with a response, 'Lord, graciously hear us', with a concluding prayer and Amen. For British Roman Catholics, David Konstant's *Bidding Prayers for the Church's Year* is an example of the variety which this freedom allows.

In the Church of England the intercessions at the eucharist were in the prayer which came to be called 'The Church Militant' prayer, and seems to have been derived from extracting the intercessions from the canon of the Mass, suggestions from Hermann von Wied, and applying Reformed principles to their scope. It was said by the priest alone. With Series 1 it was broken into paragraphs with responses, and then through the various experimental services, there were biddings, litanies and brief prayers with provision for free prayer. The 1980 ASB allows a variety of forms, and even more forms are provided for in the American *Book of Common Prayer* (1979), and in the English Methodist book of 1975. The American *Lutheran Book of Worship* provides only the themes, giving considerable freedom.

The URC draft forms in the 1970s provided a litany as well as prayers in paragraphs, but in the final form as found in 1980 the litany form disappeared. No forms were provided in 1989. A variety of forms appear in the three eucharistic orders of the Church of Scotland *Book of Common Order* (1979).

Generally it is in the intercessions where most freedom is allowed to the minister or ministers, and here quite common mistakes are made: biddings are made, but no prayer is actually addressed to God; many subjects of the prayers are simply lifted out of the newspapers; the leader cannot be heard; the themes are sometimes exclusive or someone's private political agenda; they are often didactic, telling the congregation what they ought to know rather than asking anything of God; they are often too verbose. One new development which is often quite helpful is to link the theme of some of the intercessions with the lections and sermon.

The shape of the eucharistic action

It is perhaps easiest to begin with the Anglican rites. Modern Anglican revision cannot be understood without appreciating the influence of Gregory Dix. Dix argued that a seven action shape at the Last Supper was condensed by the early Church to a four-fold action – taking, thanksgiving, breaking and communion. This was the main thesis of the great tome, *The Shape of the Liturgy* (1945). It was from this premise that the format or structure of 1552–1662 was criticized.

However, although these four actions – so useful in confirmation classes! – have dominated Anglican liturgical thinking, criticism has been forthcoming. To begin with, Dix was not good at maths, because at the Last Supper there were nine actions, not seven (Dix missed the all-important interpretive words). Dr G. Michel questioned Dix's final total, pointing out that the four actions were not of equal importance. Taking and breaking were purely utilitarian actions, having no primary theological significance.[6] These criticisms were acknowledged by the JLG in their *Initiation*

[6] G. Michel, *Landmarks in Liturgy*, 1961.

and Eucharist, where it was conceded that the eucharist is basically two actions – thanksgiving, with eating and drinking.[7]

The Parish and People movement espoused Dix's theory, and put a great deal of emphasis on the offertory procession, representing the offering to God of our toil and work. This was criticized by Archbishop Michael Ramsey as shallow and romantic pelagianism. In the ASB there has been a certain amount of climb-down on the offertory, but not enough. There is the 'Preparation of the gifts' which is now separated from the 'Taking of the bread and wine'. One wonders whether in any revision it would be better to group these rubrics around the thanksgiving rather than to fiddle with prayers and the words from 1 Chr. 29:11 and 16, or implicitly allow the Roman Catholic prayers which are less than ideal (see below). Dix's theory has been influential in the *Lutheran Book of Worship*, as well as in practically all other Anglican revisions.

The Roman Catholic rite has not been wedded to the same theory. The offertory prayers of the Tridentine Mass were, in fact, mainly Gallican and Mozarabic in origin. They pointed forward to the canon of the Mass, but the language of some of them anticipated the offering in the canon so much that the prayers were known as the 'Little canon'. In 1965 it was proposed to remove or reduce these prayers to a minimum, and to use the following at the taking of the bread and wine respectively:

> As this bread was scattered and then gathered and made one,
> so may your Church be gathered into your kingdom.
> Glory to you, God, for ever.
>
> Wisdom has built a house for herself,
> she has mixed her wine,
> she has set her table.
> Glory to you, for ever.

[7] Bryan D. Spinks, 'Mis-Shapen, Gregory Dix and the Four-Action Shape of the Liturgy', *Lutheran Quarterly*, 4 (1990), pp. 161–71.

Between 1965 and 1968 a number of schemes were put forward. The final form are two *berakah*-style prayers (Blessed are you, Lord God . . .) and the retention of two prayers from the 'Little canon'. The anticipation of the offering in the eucharistic prayer is toned down, but not entirely eliminated. The rite does not make anything of great importance of the fraction, though it remains a distinct action.

The URC 1980 rite did have a four-fold shape, but it perhaps owes as much to the Calvinist tradition as to Dix. A short prayer linking the gifts (ambiguous as to whether it is money or the bread and wine) to the offering of the sacrifice of praise and self-offering is followed by the narrative of institution as a warrant, and the taking of the bread and cup is done in obedience to the narrative, with an emphasis on thanksgiving over the bread and wine. The fraction is accompanied by a reading of the institution narrative or 1 Cor. 10:16–17, which has a long precedent reaching back to the Puritan liturgies of the sixteenth and seventeenth centuries. The 1989 book adopts the Roman *berakah* prayers and adds a new one, thus putting more emphasis on the offertory. The Scottish *Book of Common Order* 1979 follows the tradition of 1940, based on the Eastern rites. There is a prayer of the veil, the Creed, then the Reformed warrant.

The English Methodist rite has the setting of the table as a heading, with appropriate rubrics, but no prayers or declarations accompany the action, thus actually highlighting a three-fold shape of thanksgiving, breaking and communion.

Thus, in the different traditions we find different emphases on the taking or preparing the bread and wine, and the significance of the fraction.

The eucharistic prayer

The Liturgical Movement has resulted in a growing consensus on the eucharistic prayer. Most denominations have compiled new eucharistic prayers (EPs) modelled upon the 'classical' shape of the fourth and fifth centuries; and most denominations have provided a number of eucharistic prayers from which the celebrant may choose. The Roman rite has four (plus three for children, two for reconciliation, and, since 1991, one for 'various occasions'); the Church of England ASB has four; the American Prayer Book of 1979 has four in Rite 2; the URC 1980 rite has three. The English Methodist 1975 rite stands out as an exception in that it provided a single eucharistic prayer. Some denominations have included updated versions of their own distinctive historic forms – the *Lutheran Book of Worship* provides for a form based upon Luther's rites; the Church of England ASB includes a 1662 Prayer Book pattern of prayer of consecration; and the 1989 URC rite provides an order with separate prayers over the bread and wine representing the usage of the Churches of Christ.

Looking at the new prayers adopting the 'classical' shape, a number of features stand out:

1. The *Apostolic Tradition* attributed to Hippolytus has been influential – perhaps to the point of nausea. EP 2 of the Roman rite was inspired by this prayer, as were in differing degrees EPs 1, 2 and 3 of the ASB. It has inspired prayers in a variety of American denominations' rites. Only the URC seems to have resisted the magnetism of this prayer, and perhaps wisely, since a number of more recent studies have questioned how normative the anaphora of Hippolytus actually was.

2. EP 1 of the Roman rite is a revision of the old Roman canon. Prayer 4 was inspired by the Egyptian version of St Basil; scholars disagree over the immediate inspiration of EP 3, some suggesting a Mozarabic/Gallican inspiration, others suggesting an Alexandrine model. The West Syrian pattern has been influential in most denominations – particularly the American and Canadian Anglican rites, and the American Methodist and

Presbyterain rites, and the Church of Scotland. However, no really sound argument has been advanced as to why West Syrian fifth-century forms should be the basis for twentieth-century prayers.

3. The West Syrian custom of a congregational response or acclamation at the anamnesis has been partly imitated in the new rites. A congregational response is given, but in the Roman Catholic, Church of England and English Methodist rites it comes immediately after the institution narrative. The Joint Liturgical Group EP and the American Prayer Book of 1979 EPs follow the authentic West Syrian position of placing it after the anamnesis passage.

4. All the prayers have included the Sanctus – though it is omitted in the ASB additional Eucharistic Prayer for the sick. Because the Sanctus has become a traditional chant, the *Apostolic Tradition*, which does not use it, could not be used as it stands. However, few Churches seem to have given much thought to the use and function of the Sanctus. The Church of England Series 2 was composed with E. C. Ratcliff's theory in mind, that it could come at the end; three prayers of the English Congregationalist rite of 1970 concluded with the Sanctus. Otherwise, it appears to have been inserted simply because people expected it to be there. However, what is noticeable in most new rites is a very restrained angelological introduction, reflecting twentieth-century unease with angelology.[8]

5. The general sequence of thanksgiving is for creation and redemption, though the emphasis is always on redemption.

6. Following long-established Calvinist custom, URC rites still provide for the narrative to be recited as a warrant and omitted from the EP.

[8] Bryan D. Spinks, *The Sanctus in the Eucharistic Prayer*, CUP, Cambridge, 1991.

7. The Holy Spirit has been given a proper place in the EPs, both by rehearsing his role in salvation history and by the inclusion of a petition for the Spirit to be involved in the communion. Its precise formulation differs widely. The English Methodist rite has a petition after the narrative that by the power of the Spirit those who receive the gifts of bread and wine may share in the body and blood of Christ. The *Alternative Service Book* EPs have a petition before the narrative, asking that through the power of the Spirit the gifts 'may be to us the body and blood of Christ' – a form which goes back to 1549 and 1637. At least since the seventeenth century the Calvinist rites have had a petition for the Spirit, and thus the URC and Church of Scotland have forms of epiclesis.

The new Roman EPs have a double epiclesis – one before the narrative which is concerned with the elements, and one after which is concerned for the communicants. There is no real historical precedent for this arrangement, but it seems to be a combination of the forms found in two Egyptian fragments together with the older Roman *Quam oblationem* and *Supplices te*. This has been criticized by Catholic scholars as turning the eucharistic prayer into settings for consecration of the elements. Richard Albertine writes:

> Unfortunately the epiklesis solution employed in the three new eucharistic prayers brings with it two major negative effects:
>
> 1. The proclamation of the events of salvation history is unevenly represented largely due to the epiklesis arrangement.
>
> 2. The double epiklesis format tends to reinforce the consecratory section setting off the institution account from the cursus of the anaphora.[9]

[9] Richard Albertine, 'Problem of the (Double) Epiclesis in the New Roman Eucharistic Prayers', *Ephemerides Liturgicae*, 99 (1977), pp. 193–202. For the American prayers, see J. H. McKenna, 'The Epiclesis Revisited. A look at Modern Eucharistic Prayers', *Empherides Liturgicae*, 99 (1985), pp. 314–36.

8. Finally, much controversy has raged around the problem of offering and eucharistic sacrifice. It was most dramatic in the Church of England where Colin Buchanan dissented from the draft form of Series 2 because the EP contained the words 'we offer unto thee this bread and this cup'. It was subsequently rephrased as: 'with this bread and cup we make the memorial', which led to A. H. Couratin's resignation on academic grounds. Only with Series 3 and the subsequent ASB was a more happy compromise reached between Evangelicals and Anglo-Catholics.

In the Roman EPs, traditional offering language has been retained, with the bread and cup being offered. However, almost in contradiction to the teaching of Thomas Aquinas and Trent, EP 4 offers 'his body and blood, the acceptable sacrifice which brings salvation to the whole world'.[10]

One problem seems to be the relationship Churches envisage between *lex orandi* and *lex credendi*. The 1970 English Congregationalist rite provided six eucharistic prayers, each with a differently articulated anamnesis, including the controversial phraseology which Colin Buchanan could not accept on behalf of Anglican Evangelicals. The reason was that Congregationalist theology was not tied to or dictated by its liturgical forms. The Worship Committee was therefore happy to present a range of different terminology in the anamnesis. The Roman Catholic Church can argue that whatever is in its liturgical forms, it must ultimately be interpreted in the light of the teaching of the Church. Here Anglicans have had difficulty, because many of them have tried to insist that its doctrine can be found in its liturgical forms, almost turning liturgy into a creed.

Naïvely, perhaps, we might suggest that ultimately, whether in the anamnesis we offer, celebrate, call to mind,

[10] For a full discussion, see K. W. Stevenson, *Eucharist*.

remember, make the memorial, present the sign of faith, bring before God the gifts, or, as in the Church of Scotland, plead his eternal sacrifice, it does not much matter provided it does not become the source of doctrinal speculation, and provided it is done in, with and through Christ. The concluding doxology is far from an appendage; it anchors all we do in the self-offering of Christ.

Selected Reading

C. J. Cocksworth, *Evangelical Eucharistic Thought in the Church of England*, Cambridge, Cambridge University Press, 1993.

William R. Crocket, *Eucharist: Symbol of Transformation*, New York, Pueblo, 1989.

Peter C. Finn and James M. Schellman (eds), *Shaping English Liturgy*, Washington, Pastoral Press, 1990.

Frank C. Senn (ed.), *New Eucharistic Prayers*, New York, Paulist Press, 1987.

K. W. Stevenson (ed.), *Liturgy Reshaped*, London, SPCK, 1982.

— *Eucharist and Offering*, New York, Pueblo, 1986.

Studia Liturgica, 22 (1992) contains papers on the Bible in the liturgy and lectionary discussion.

13

The Changing Face of Baptism and Confirmation

Christian initiation has four important theological dimensions: soteriological – washing of sin; Christological – putting on the Lord Jesus; pneumatological – the gift of the Spirit, which distinguished the Christian rite from that of John the Baptist; and ecclesiological – the candidate becomes a member of the people of God. However, when it comes to the liturgical articulation of these, there has been disagreement between Churches and within Churches about to whom, what and how. These questions have dominated theological and liturgical discussion over the last fifty years.

To whom? The problem of infant baptism

Although the thrust of New Testament evangelism was towards adults, from the fourth century onwards the number of infants being baptized increased to a point where in many areas the only candidates were the children of Christian parents. It was the application to infants of exorcisms designed for adults which helped Augustine to develop his powerful doctrine of original sin and guilt, with dire warnings on the fate of those who died unbaptized. As a direct result baptism of infants within a week became a requirement in the Western Church. The medieval Church and the majority of the Reformation Churches inherited Augustinian theology where baptism was primarily a rite of cleansing. This was challenged in the sixteenth century by the Anabaptists, who insisted on personal faith and therefore rejected infant baptism. Apart from their successors in the Baptist Church and some Evangelical Churches, the majority of Churches in the West accepted paedobaptism, though defending it on grounds of vicarious faith (Luther) or a form of covenant theology (Zwingli, Calvin).

In the 1940s controversy raged in continental theology over whether infant baptism was justified, with Brunner, Barth and Aland coming out against infant baptism, and Jeremias, Cullmann, Leenhardt and Marcel defending the practice. Barth, for example, argued that there is no such thing as infant baptism, but only baptism, and its criteria (baptism was the human response to the divine grace) ruled out infant candidates; Jeremias, on the other hand, argued that since the New Testament refers to the baptism of households, this must have included infants, citing much early Church evidence in favour of this conclusion. It would be wrong to see this as simply a debate between the giants of the academic world. It resulted from observations that in European societies many people brought their children for baptism, but neither they nor the children were actively taking up their Christian status.

In the Church of England, already in a report on Poplar (London) in 1939, grave doubts were voiced about 'indiscriminate' baptism, and the report recommended the tightening up of instruction of parents applying for their child's baptism, and even deferring the sacrament in families whose older children were not going to church. This concern was repeated in reports in 1944, 1949, 1954, and the famous Swanwick Ecumenical Conference, Crisis for Baptism, 1965. Those who were suspicious of infant baptism could point out that baptism of households in the New Testament implied committed adults who would bring up children in the faith; the objection was not so much to infant baptism, as to indiscriminate baptism. Those who defended the *status quo* could appeal to prevenient grace. At a pastoral and liturgical level it has meant asking questions as to whether all baptisms should be at a public service, whether godparents should be vetted and whether the parents should undergo instruction. In some quarters it was suggested that only infants of committed Christians should be baptized, and that the normal liturgical rite should be adult baptism and confirmation and communion in one rite.

It is true that in England it was an Anglican problem. However, in Scotland it was a Presbyterian problem, discussed in full reports to the General Assembly from 1955 to 1962, and subsequently; and in France it was a Roman Catholic problem, discussed in full by scholars such as A. M. Roguet and A. G. Martimont, who both attacked indiscriminate baptism. Where there has been a majority Church or an established Church, infant baptism was being used by many of the populace who had themselves no commitment to the Church.

What and how? The problem of confirmation

In the early centuries, although there may have been preparation for baptism, the liturgical rite was one. However, in the West infant baptism became detached from the episcopal hand-laying and anointing in the rite, which became known as confirmation, and was generally reserved for the bishop. At first it was delayed by months, and then years.[1] For the Reformers the word 'confirmation' meant a mature confession of faith – the adult acceptance of what had been promised by parents or godparents, whereas for many medieval theologians it was regarded as a separate sacrament completing baptism.

On the whole it has been in the Anglican Church where confirmation has been most fiercely debated, though in the last twenty-five years at least, a debate has been going on in the Roman Catholic Church, and some Lutheran Churches.

[1] Fisher, *Christian Initiation; Confirmation Then and Now.*

In this century the debate began in earnest in 1946 with the publication of Gregory Dix's *The Theology of Confirmation in Relation to Baptism*. In this book Dix argued that baptism forgives sins, regenerates us and joins us to the Body of Christ, but it is left for confirmation to bestow the actual indwelling of the Holy Spirit. Initiation is therefore not complete without confirmation, which may indeed be regarded as the more important of the two. Such a position had been argued at the end of the nineteenth century by A. J. Mason, and so this view is often described as the Mason–Dix view. It was also defended by L. S. Thornton.

A very different view was argued by G. W. Lampe in 1951 in *The Seal of the Spirit*. He sifted the early evidence, and concluded that for the early Church baptism in water was the only rite known, and the Holy Spirit was imparted though the baptism in water. Confirmation was a rite in which:

> the Christian who was baptized in infancy was now able to make his necessary profession of faith after due instruction, and, on so supplying the deficiency which infant baptism would otherwise suffer, to receive the blessing of the representative leader of the Christian society with prayer for his strengthening and increase in the Holy Spirit.[2]

Much of the debate is centred on references in the Acts of the Apostles, and the meaning of laying on of hands in Luke–Acts.

The books by Dix and Lampe summed up the two interpretations of confirmation in the Anglican Church, and the official reports produced during 1948–71 swung as a pendulum from one view to another. A theological and liturgical debate ensued between England's two foremost experts on baptismal liturgy, J. D. C. Fisher arguing from a Dixian view, and E. C. Whitaker representing the Lampe view.

[2] Lampe, *The Seal of the Spirit*, London, SPCK, 2nd edn., 1967, p. 134.

Meanwhile, the Ely Report of 1971 (with Lampe as a member of the committee) declared that baptism should be recognized as the full and complete rite of Christian initiation. Confirmation would continue, but it could be administered by either the bishop or a minister appointed by him, and would not be part of initiation, but a service of commitment or commissioning. A logical extension of this view was put forward in the Knaresborough Report, *Communion Before Confirmation?* (1985) which suggested that baptized children should be admitted to communion before confirmation.

The Church of England has so far not acted on either of these reports, but elsewhere in the Anglican Communion such as New Zealand, the USA, Canada and Scotland, initiation is regarded as complete in baptism, and confirmation is not a prerequisite of admission to communion. This view was urged to be adopted by all Anglican Provinces by the International Anglican Liturgical Consultation at Boston in 1985, and more forcefully at Toronto in 1991, though it is still being resisted by the bishops of the Church of England, 'the last bastion of resistance to change'.[3]

In the Roman Catholic Church there has also been a questioning of confirmation. In 1910 Pope Pius X decided to encourage children to receive communion at the age of 7, and as a result it became common for children to be prepared for confession and admitted to communion before confirmation, which was administered by a bishop at the age of 12. Whatever confirmation might confer, it was necessary for communion. Some writers suggested that it was a lay ordination to the active ministry of the Church; others argued that it might become repeatable at key moments of one's passage through life. Most recently Professor Aidan Kavanagh has argued that the laying on of hands was really only a 'missa', an episcopal blessing into the assembly, though its association with the Holy Spirit has

[3] Holeton (ed.), *Growing in Newness of Life.*

been defended by Frank Quinn.[4] This debate has continued despite Pope Paul VI's bull *Divinium consortium naturae* of 1971 which asserted that confirmation was the completion of initiation endowing the candidate with the Holy Spirit.

A side issue in this debate about the meaning of confirmation in episcopal Churches has been whether or not the rite can be delegated. In the Roman Catholic Church it may now be delegated to a presbyter; in spite of good theological arguments to follow suit, Anglican bishops reserved this rite for themselves, apparently in fear of being marginalized rather than for any convincing theological reason.

Some characteristics of the new rites of initiation

Unlike the new eucharistic liturgies, there is far less agreement in structure and texts in the new baptismal rites of the various Churches: the trinitarian formula in the traditional Western active tense ('I baptize you . . .') and possibly the Lord's Prayer are usually the only common forms. However, a number of trends can be detected.

The adoption of the 'Patristic Model' of initiation as the norm

Many Churches have opted for a model of initiation which reflects that found in the catechetical lectures of Fathers such as Cyril of Jerusalem, Ambrose and John Chrysostom, where the ideal or norm is a rite for adults which unites baptism, confirmation and communion. This is so in the ASB 1980, and even more forcefully in the elaborate Roman Catholic Rite of Christian Initiation for Adults (RCIA). Other rites such as baptism of adults without confirmation, or confirmation without the eucharist, are presented as derived rites from the norm. The 1980 URC book provided an order for infant baptism first, and then an order for the baptism and confirmation of adults. In the 1989 book a single rite is

[4] Kavanagh, *Confirmation*; Quinn, *Worship*, 59 (1985), pp. 354–70.

offered with provision through parallel texts for adaptation for either infants or adults. Confirmation remains as a separate rite presumably intended for those baptized in infancy.

Since in a post-Christian world there are a significant (and increasing) number of adults who come to faith and have not been baptized in infancy, the patristic rites have been used to develop a set of stage rites in Rites of Christian Initiation for Adults (RCIA). These treat faith as a gradual coming to the gospel and faith, and provide for the catechumenate, and a series of rites to celebrate the maturing of faith, culminating in baptism, confirmation and communion. These rites have been influential in the rites for the catechumenate developed in the Episcopal Church of America, and in the programme developed by Canon Peter Ball in England.

A move away from an 'Augustinian' concern with sin to a 'Cyprianic' concern for incorporation in the Church

This is seen in a number of different ways in the different denominations. Whereas in the Anglican Prayer Book rite there is mention of being conceived and born in sin, and to mystical washing and deliverance, in the ASB the dominant theme is being received into the 'family of the Church' and the promises centre on bringing the child up as an active member of the Church. In the Roman Catholic rite of infant baptism the exorcism and renunciation of Satan have been considerably reduced, with an emphasis on welcoming the child into the Church. The same emphasis is found in the Methodist rite of 1975, and the URC rites of 1980 and 1989. Of course the concept of sin, and the devil (or evil) is still present, but there is undoubtedly a shift of emphasis.

An unconscious adoption of the early Reformed emphasis on the role of parents rather than godparents at the baptism of infants

Until 1969 the Roman Catholic Church used a single baptismal rite which, though used mainly for infants, was a compressed form of an order once used over a period of time for adults. In 1969 for the first time it produced a rite of baptism specifically for infants. In the rite itself the duty of parents is stressed. Likewise in the Church of England, the ASB rite asks for undertakings from parents, and the renunciations and promises are addressed to parents as well as godparents. Hitherto the 'catholic' tradition of baptism had placed an emphasis on godparents, not parents.

With this has developed (again unconsciously) an implicit acceptance of the covenant theology of the Reformation, which emphasizes baptism as a mutual covenant between God and humans rather than emphasizing it as a sacrament of prevenient grace. The two are not, of course, necessarily exclusive. Nevertheless, the stress in current Church of England, Methodist, Church of Scotland and Roman Catholic debate and pastoral guidelines puts an emphasis on parental conditions before infants are baptized, which was the position of many of the Reformed theologians of the late sixteenth and early seventeenth centuries.

Involvement of the whole Church

Baptism is entry into the Christian community, and there has been a move away from private baptism to baptism within a normal act of worship. In the service the congregation is given a part to play. Thus, in the 1975 Methodist rite the minister says to the congregation:

> Members of the Body of Christ, who are now in his name to receive this child, will you so maintain the common life of worship and service that he and all the children among you may grow in grace and in knowledge and love of God and of his Son Jesus Christ our Lord?

The 1989 URC rite asks:

> Do you, as members of Christ's body and trusting in God's grace, promise to pray for A. . . , provide for the teaching of the gospel, and live a Christian life in the family of God?

In the Roman Catholic rite for infant baptism, and in the Church of England rite, the congregation give their consent to the profession of faith, and the latter also includes a congregational welcome. RCIA envisages members of the congregation befriending and instructing adult catechumens.

A concern for symbolism

Some of the new rites of baptism encourage ministers to make more use of water during the baptism itself. Pouring and immersion are encouraged rather than sprinkling, to show that the font is at the heart of the rite. Other symbolism is the use of a candle given to represent the light of Christ, provided for now also by the URC rite of 1989.

Another traditional symbol has been oil. Here the Church of England has given us an example of bad symbolism. Oil still ought to be a self-evident symbol for those who call themselves after the Anointed One. Some Churches have been suspicious of its use since in some traditions the anointing has been sacramental, and has even eclipsed the significance of baptism in water. Originally it was decided not to include it in the revised Church of England rite, and so no rubrics or formulae were prepared for its use. At the last minute a rubric was inserted at the beginning of the service allowing oil to be used with the sign of the cross (normally just traced with the thumb) before or after the baptism, and at confirmation. However, since nothing in the service actually mentions oil, its use seems quite pointless. It really is a 'dumb ceremony'. It could, however, be a powerful symbol of Christian allegiance, and messianic status.

Confirmation and infant communion

The problem over confirmation outlined earlier has not been resolved. In the Protestant tradition it remains an act of commitment for adults and young teenagers who were baptized in infancy, and the means of admittance to communicant status. In some Anglican Provinces it is an act of commitment made after instruction, making good the lack of personal profession at infant baptism, and the means of admission to communion; in others, it is all these, but children baptized as babies are admitted to communion by virtue of their baptism. In all cases, it is still administered only by the bishop. In the Roman Catholic Church it is still regarded as sacramental, but may be delegated to the priest. Although the norm is baptism, confirmation, communion, even if separated by time, in practice in many countries first communion still takes place before confirmation. Some Protestant Churches – for example the Church of Scotland – are now beginning to allow the admission of baptized infants to communion status.

'Rebaptism'

All orthodox Churches acknowledge that there is only one baptism, and it cannot be repeated. The use of an ecumenically agreed and recognized certificate of baptism is a helpful step to affirm this belief. However, there are an increasing number of people who, although baptized as infants, had no church upbringing at all, and have come into the Church as adults. They often want to mark their 'conversion' with baptism. At present the Churches are having to consider what liturgical form they can offer such people which will meet their spiritual and psychological needs without denying the reality and validity of their infant baptism.

Selected Reading

Colin Buchanan, *One Baptism Once*, Grove Booklet 61, Bramcote, Grove Books, 3rd edn., 1987.

— *Infant Baptism and the Gospel*, London, Darton, Longman & Todd, 1993.

Sandra DeGidio, *RCIA: The Rites Revisited*, Minneapolis, Winston Press, 1984.

J. D. C. Fisher, *Christian Initiation: Baptism in the Medieval West*, London, Alcuin Club/SPCK, 1965.

— *Confirmation Then and Now*, London, Alcuin Club/SPCK, 1978.

David S. M. Hamilton, *Through the Waters*, Edinburgh, T & T Clark, 1990.

David R. Holeton (ed.), *Growing in Newness of Life, Christian initiation in Anglicanism today*. Toronto, Anglican Book Centre, 1993.

A. Kavanagh, *The Shape of Baptism*, New York, Pueblo, 1978.

— *Confirmation: Origins and Reform*, New York, Pueblo, 1988.

Max Thurian (ed.), *Ecumenical Perspectives on Baptism. Eucharist and Ministry*, Geneva, World Council of Churches, 1983.

Arthur S. Yates, *Why Baptize Infants?*, Norwich, Canterbury Press, 1993.

14

The Language of Worship

Few areas of liturgical change in the second half of the twentieth century have produce such violent reactions as that of the language of worship. It has been a major contributory factor to division within Churches and has left some worshippers feeling cut off from the roots of their faith. For others changes in language have been a clear gospel imperative and a powerful enabler in the Church's mission. The question of human language has always been bound up with the history of the Church. In large measure this is the result of two 'poles' in Christianity. The one pole is the Book which contains God's definitive self-revelation, recorded predominantly in two languages: Hebrew of the Semitic family and Indo-European Greek. The other pole is the Church's conviction that it is under an obligation to communicate that revelation to the people of all cultures, languages and centuries. There is thus a built-in tension between the unchanging 'deposit' and the ever-widening number of languages and contexts into which it is to be intelligibly communicated. Similarly, Christians from many diverse language groups need to be able to respond in worship in a manner that is a genuine expression of their faith and yet also relates to the definitive deposit. The issue, clearly, is not a new one. However, it has emerged in a particularly self-conscious and acute form in parts of the World Church as a second to third generation issue in the Liturgical Movement.

Christianity has never had a sacred language as such. Jesus was soaked in the Hebrew Scriptures yet taught in the vernacular Aramaic. His words were written down in Greek – a language of a totally different type – yet one which had a far greater currency in the whole of the Roman Empire than Aramaic.

Where Greek would suffice, Greek was used. Soon, however, the Church began to penetrate areas and groups in society where other languages predominated, and began to use them accordingly. Translations of the Scriptures into Syriac, Armenian, Latin and Gothic soon began. The story cannot be told in detail here but the evidence shows that in most cases, particularly in the East, the vernacular was soon adopted for worship. The survival of abundant ancient liturgical texts in Coptic, Syriac and Armenian, for example, is clear testimony to this. Only in the Western Church was the situation rather different. Here, Latin remained something of a *lingua franca* in a Western Europe and North Africa fragmented by numerous 'barbarian' tongues. Moreover Latin was the vernacular in Rome which for historical and, increasingly, dogmatic reasons sought to play a centralizing role in the Western Church.

Languages change or are slowly abandoned. The issue is whether or at what pace the language of liturgy should reflect the changes (or even initiate them). The Greek of the Byzantine rite is now largely unintelligible to modern Greeks. The same is true of Old Slavonic in modern Russia. In Egypt, Coptic has not been a living language for several centuries, yet remains the language of much of the worship of the Church. For societies such as these, however, changing the language of worship is far from the relatively straightforward process of continued updating that some Western Christians would seem to suggest. For all peoples, but perhaps especially for the Churches of Eastern Europe and the Middle East, liturgical language is closely bound up with the issues of continuity, ethnic and religious identity and authority. Furthermore, in most of these Churches the worshippers do not have any texts in their hands at all. The liturgy is known by heart through constant repetition. Changing the words in such a situation (especially if literacy levels are low) is far from easy. Indeed the very idea would be unacceptable still in many quarters: the liturgy is a drama handed down by the Fathers. To 'modernize' it would be like putting Shakespeare into modern English and letting the actors perform it with the scripts in their hands. From this perspective much of the contemporary debate about liturgical language is a dangerous exercise irresponsibly indulged in by highly privileged sections of the Church. While such a perspective may have elements of truth in it, it is itself clearly a distortion. There *are* genuine issues of theology and principles involved in the question of liturgical language. To many the credibility and evangelistic impact of the Church is also at stake.

For Christians in the English-speaking world the issue was first encountered in the question of using 'thee' and 'thou' forms in worship. This form of the second person singular (a characteristic shared with many other languages) was widespread in the sixteenth and seventeenth centuries and came to be incorporated in the liturgies, hymns and prayer forms deriving from that and subsequent periods. Gradually however the 'thou' form was lost from standard English and vernacular speech (with some dialect exceptions), being replaced by the plural 'you' form. Thus, by the mid-twentieth century most English speakers encountered 'thou' form English only in church. The old vernacular had become by association a hieratic language, the only correct form for addressing God. (This is clearly demonstrated by the fact that until perhaps the 1960s extempore prayer by ministers and laity, both in church and in less formal settings, was in 'thou' form.) It was forgotten that, although Cranmer did indeed address God as 'thou', he also called Mrs Cranmer 'thou' and his horse 'thou'.

Interestingly, earlier generations had been more open to change. Cranmer, of course, had pioneered the transition from Latin to English in the 1540s and early 1550s, pointing out that St Paul would 'have such language spoken to the people in the Church, as they might understand and have profit by hearing the same'.[1]

Just over a century later, Cranmer's own handiwork was ripe for some linguistic revision. The preface to the 1662 Book of Common Prayer states,

> . . . as to the several variations from the former Book most of the alterations were made either first, for the better observation of them that are to officiate . . . or secondly, for the more proper expressing of some words or phrases of ancient usage in terms more suitable to the language of the present times, and the clearer explanation of some other works and phrases that were either of doubtful signification, or otherwise liable to misconstruction.

There is evidence, however, of some resistance to change. The *Durham Book* is a 1619 edition of the Prayer Book in which John Cosin, Bishop of Durham, wrote his proposed alterations in 1660–61. Some of these were incorporated into the new book of 1662. One which was not was his proposed alteration of 'Our Father which art in Heaven . . .' to 'Our Father *who* art in Heaven'. Presumably the archaic form was felt to be too familiar to change!

So firmly entrenched was 'thou' form English as the only appropriate vehicle for addressing God that both hymn writing and liturgical composition were in this form until well into the second half of the twentieth century. The Church of England's proposed 1928 Prayer Book, and its parallels in other parts of the Anglican communion were thus in Tudor English. Even when the Church of England began revising its liturgy from first principles, in the light of the insights of the Liturgical Movement, the first products of this – the Series 2 set of rites – were firmly in 'thou' form English. As recently as 1984 the Church in

[1] 'Concerning the Service of the Church', *Book of Common Prayer*, 1662.

Wales was still publishing new official texts in 'thou' form English.[2]

The decisive break came in 1971 with the publication of the draft Series 3 communion service. 'You' instead of 'thou' was used in address to God. This resulted in the loss of the verb forms associated with the singular person (hast, wast, hearest, etc.) and some re-thinking about structure and phraseology. (Turning 'Be thou mindful' into modern English demonstrates the problem. 'Be you mindful' does not 'work'; the result is that the phrase is reduced to the single word 'Remember'.) While generally welcomed, the change fuelled the debate – which still continues – on the nature of liturgical language. It was realized that there was no such thing as a single form of 'modern English'. Spoken language differs from written language; should the language used be that of the 'popular press' or that of the 'quality press' (the *Sun* or *The Times*?). Should it be plain and functional or poetic, allusive and dignified?

In addition to the wider debate there were specific issues about what form liturgical items which were used in more than one tradition should take. It was felt to be highly undesirable that Methodists might use one form of the Lord's Prayer, for example, while Anglicans used another. At the local level Christians of different Churches were beginning to attend each others services or participate in joint acts of worship. It would clearly be unfortunate if the use of different forms of common texts and prayers made the division between them even harder to overcome.

Fortunately action was taken which did in fact minimize this potential danger. The Roman Catholic International Commission on English in the Liturgy (ICEL) – formed to supervise the production of English forms of the post-Vatican II liturgical texts – was broadened in 1969 into the International Consultation on English Texts (ICET) and

[2] To look at the demise of this form of English in the Anglican Communion, see C. O. Buchanan's series *Modern English Liturgies, Further Liturgies* and *Latest Anglican Liturgies*.

produced *Prayers We Have in Common* in 1970 (revised in 1971 and 1975). Standard English forms of the Creeds, the *Gloria in Excelsis, Te Deum,* etc. were produced and widely used by many Churches as they revised their rites into modern English (with some local modifications). The Lord's Prayer has proved particularly difficult to render satisfactorily, but a widely used form has prevailed. ICET – now succeeded by the English Language Liturgical Consultation (ELLC) – has continued to revise the texts in keeping with further developments in the understanding of liturgical language. Its latest set, published as *Praying Together*, appeared in 1988.[3]

Much debate has centred on the effect that modern language has had on theology and piety. It has been argued that, for example, the gravity of sin and of the gulf between God and us is obscured by modern form of the General Confession: '. . . a brief apology couched in the terms of mild regret appropriate to a minor traffic offence is hardly an adequate expression of the profound sinfulness of our condition.'[4] The confession in the Church of England's Series 2 Communion Service did not even mention sorrow for sin; an omission which was rectified in Series 3.

Part of this concern relates to the *depth* of modern liturgical language. By definition it is going to have to bear frequent repetition. Does the poetry, imagery and structure make it memorable? Will it provide a constant source of mental, emotional and spiritual nourishment to worshippers over the years, or will it rapidly become threadbare and bankrupt? There are indeed signs that a gentle reaction to the simplifications of liturgical language has already begun. England in the 1970s saw the production of a series of rites which achieved official status in the ASB of the Church of England in 1980. Since then, however, much of the Liturgical Commission's work has consisted in the production of texts

[3] *Praying Together*, Norwich, Canterbury Press, 1988.

[4] Sermon preached by Adrian Leake in York Minster on 25 September 1984.

which enrich and enhance this earlier provision. Both in language and content works like *Lent, Holy Week and Easter* (1986). *Patterns for Worship* (1989) and *Promise of His Glory* (1991) are more poetic, more allusive and verbally richer than the ASB. It will be interesting to see whether a widespread strong turning of the tide takes place. Allied to this is the issue of how many of Christianity's technical terms should be retained. Should a new worshipper be able to comprehend everything from the beginning, or should there be an expectation that a new vocabulary will accompany a growth in faith and commitment? The demand for total intelligibility is questioned in some quarters: anyone seeking to master a home computer or understand a car engine will accept the necessity of learning new words and procedures. Why should doing so present such a problem in the Church?

There is a further aspect in which liturgical language in the 1980s and beyond differs radically from that of the 1970s. Since about 1980 the English-speaking world (or at least parts of it) has been caught up in the so-called inclusive language debate. This is an issue which both reflects and feeds on important sociological shifts in perception as well as incorporating insights from within Christianity itself. Indeed the very dichotomy suggested by stating the situation in that way would be rejected by some. The issue is a far-reaching one and, like other areas, only the main outlines can be sketched here.

The twentieth century has seen a marked change in the position and perception of women within West European and North American culture. As this is currently the dominant world culture, the changed position of women is reflected in varying degrees in other parts of the world. (This is not to suggest that it is solely a First World development or that Christianity has not necessarily anything to do with it. On the contrary, the Church in many parts of the world has been – for biblical reasons – a major promoter of the alleviation of the situation of women.) English, like most languages of the Indo-European family (and indeed other families), uses for mixed groups and for representative individuals inclusive terms which happen to be identical with the form used for the male:

> 'One of the greatest threats that man has to grapple with . . .'
> 'Through his studies, the student will be enabled to . . .'

In some instances this is the result of a gradually restricting use of generic terms: 'mann' referred to both sexes in Old English and has only over the centuries come to be thought to apply solely to the male. Some would maintain that the language conventions are themselves the product of societies predominantly patriarchal in structure and assumptions. The language therefore reflects a sociology which is itself challenged by some advocates of inclusive language. (Whether patriarchy is a God-given feature of human society is an issue which awaits deep and prolonged study. The answer clearly has implications for other areas of Christian life, notably the ordination of women debate.)

Whatever the origins of the linguistic forms, the fact is that generic terms which are identical with the masculine forms are no longer acceptable to some English-speaking Christians. Liturgy, which has the power to teach and shape minds, is therefore required to be recast in forms of English which are more truly 'inclusive' of female and male. At one level this is relatively straightforward. Rubrics referring to the minister leading the service should no longer read: 'he shall say . . .' The Nicene Creed can be put in the form 'for us and for our salvation' instead of 'for us men and for our salvation'. The confession: 'We have sinned against you and against our fellow men' becomes 'We have sinned against you and our neighbour'. The problem becomes more complex when the language of the Bible itself is examined. Since most liturgical language is drawn from the Scriptures, this is clearly a major determinative of the form of liturgical language. Hebrew and Greek use masculine forms of generic and representative when referring to human beings. At times English translations have, in fact, gone further than the originals warrant: 'all men' has sometimes been used where 'all' stands alone in the original, for example. In some places a gentle recasting (for example, the use of the plural) when expressing biblical ideas in a liturgical text will suffice.

Much more problematic, however, is the use of masculine in reference to God. This broadly takes two forms. At one level the liturgy can enhance (both in text and lectionary) feminine imagery of God: the woman searching for the lost coin, the labour-pains of Israel's deliverance, the hen sheltering her chicks, etc. Such biblical images are a widely acceptable balancing of excessively masculine assumptions about God. Beyond that lies the question whether – since God is beyond gender – masculine terms are appropriate at all. So the New Zealand Prayer Book reads: 'The Lord is here: God's Spirit is with us', instead of 'His Spirit is with us'.

Currently there is a large range of texts, official and unofficial, exploring this dimension of liturgical language. Is 'Our Mother in Heaven . . .' acceptable? What about 'Our Parent in Heaven . . .'? How determinative is Jesus' use of Father/Son imagery in describing his relationship with God? The fact that 'Spirit' is feminine in Hebrew and that Syriac literature contains some feminine imagery in connection with the Holy Spirit has been seized on by some as a way of introducing the feminine into the Godhead in a way that is arguably safely traditional.

The issue is clearly a contentious one and is connected with many social, political and ecclesiological questions. Its outcome will be determined by other than liturgical criteria. In the meantime one of its results is to increase the sense of provisionality surrounding many liturgical texts.

Selected Reading

D. Cockerell, 'Why Language Matters', in D. Martin and P. Mullen (eds), *No Alternative: The Prayer Book Controversy*, Oxford, Basil Blackwell, 1981.

C. Idle, *Hymns in Today's Language?*, Bramcote, Grove Books, 1982.

V. Faull and J. Sinclair, *Count Us In: Inclusive Language in the Liturgy*, Bramcote, Grove Books, 1986.

D. Frost, *The Language of Series Three*, Bramcote, Grove Books, 1973.

Alvin F. Kimel Jr (ed.), *Speaking the Christian God*, Grand Rapids, Eerdmans, 1992.

J. Morley, 'The Faltering Words of Men', in M. Furlong (ed.), *Feminine and the Church*, London, SPCK, 1984.

R. R. Ruether, article 'Inclusive Language' in J. G. Davies (ed.), *A New Dictionary of Liturgy and Worship*, London, SCM, 1986.

B. Wren, 'Sexism in Hymn Language', in *News of Hymnody*, July 1983, pp. 4–8.

— *What Language Shall I Borrow?*, London, SCM, 1989.

15
Inculturation

During the last forty to fifty years there has been a growing awareness that Christianity exists in different cultural forms. The African Christianity of Ethiopia is quite distinct in ethos from Russian Orthodoxy, or Scottish Presbyterianism, and the difference is not just doctrinal. This recognition was most obvious to those who worked in the so-called 'mission fields' where, for example, the wedding ceremony presupposed by the British Methodist Church was alien to the indigenous population. Yet if this was true of marriage, how far were services like Matins and Evensong, or the eucharist, also an alien form of religious response? Was a liturgy composed for seventeenth-century England – which was already felt by many English people to be inadequate for themselves in the twentieth century – of any value in Africa or India? Exactly the same question applied to the Tridentine services of the Roman Catholic Church. There was a growing feeling that these areas needed liturgies that sprang from their own understanding and expression of the gospel.

Terminology

In official reports, books and articles on this subject there is a considerable variety of terms used, many of them being synonymous, but some writers have attempted to make subtle distinctions in definition. In Roman Catholic circles the earlier term used was adaptation, and then inculturation. Protestants preferred to use the word indigenization, though the American term contextualization seems to have superceded it. John S. Pobee, writing from a Ghanaian African context, suggested the term 'skenosis', which means a 'tenting' or indwelling.[1] The Roman Catholic theologian Anscar Chupungco, who has written extensively on this subject, has attempted to define some of the terms. In his *Cultural Adaptation of the Liturgy* (1982), he differentiated between three types of adaptation: accommodation which touches on celebrative elements as they are performed here and now by the liturgical assembly; acculturation, which results in changing the Roman rite; and inculturation which results in the reinterpretation and transformation of a pre-Christian rite in the light of Christian faith. In the more recent *Liturgies of the Future* (1989), he has added another term, creativity, which means the composition of new liturgical texts quite independently of the Roman rites.

Vatican II and the WCC on inculturation

Adaptation was recognized explicitly in the Constitution on the Sacred Liturgy, paras. 37–40. Para. 37 states:

> In matters that do not affect the faith or good of the whole community, the Church has no desire to impose a rigid uniformity, not even in the Liturgy. On the contrary, she cultivates and develops the mental and spiritual graces and gifts of the different nations and peoples. Anything at all in the peoples' customs that is not inescapably identified with superstition and error she examines favourably and, if possible, maintains whole and entire. Sometimes, indeed, she gives it a place in the Liturgy itself, provided it conforms with the principles of the true, genuine liturgical spirit.

Such adaptation had to be sanctioned by the bishops of the country, and endorsed by the Congregation for Sacred Rites.

[1] John S. Pobee, 'The Skenosis of Christian Worship in Africa', *Studia Liturgica*, 14 (1980/81), pp. 37–52.

It was perhaps no accident that in the WCC Montreal Report on Worship of the same year, there was also a section on worship and indigenization. It referred to the Report of the Theological Commission on Worship which contained the following:

> Indigenization is a principle inherent in the Christian doctrines of Creation and Redemption, and the Incarnation of the Word of God. The cultural elements, music, dance and other forms of art of any country, reflect the glory of God's creation, transformed by the process of bringing these under the judgement of Christ.

The Montreal Report concluded:

> The indigenization of Christian Worship, required in every time and place, is the offering of the created order back to God, but converted and transfigured by the redemption that is in Christ.

Christianity and culture

The relationship between Christianity and culture is difficult to define in precise terms. Jesus was born into Jewish culture which had already been subject to Hellenistic influences. The idea that resurrection was purely a Semitic belief and not influenced by Greek ideas about the soul has been shown to be wide of the mark.[2] As Christianity moved out into the Gentile world it had to decide what was essential to the gospel and what was cultural package which could be left behind. Presumably the Passover meal setting of the eucharist was abandoned as cultural, and not central to the theology of the gospel. Later, although the borders are not at all clear-cut, Daniélou was quite justified in writing about Jewish-Christian, Hellenistic and Latin theologies, reflecting the different cultural approaches to Christian theology.

[2] G. W. E. Nickelsburg, *Resurrection, Immortality, and Eternal Life in Intertestamental Judaism*, Cambridge, Mass., Harvard University Press, 1972.

In matters of liturgy, it is fairly obvious that culture and social customs have influenced the rites and ceremonies. An obvious example is marriage, with the use of the veil, ring and, in the East, crowns, all being customs taken over by the developing Christian rites, but not specifically Christian in themselves. The East Syrian eucharistic prayer of Addai and Mari is decidedly Semitic in thought-forms, and the Roman *canon missae* uses terminology from pagan cults and the Imperial court. The list could be extended.

Aspects of liturgical inculturation

Ceremonial

The development of ceremonial has a long and complex history. Much of it came from court ceremonial in the fourth century, when Christianity emerged to become a public semi-official religion, with its rites celebrated in large basilica-style buildings before a large gathering of people. Not all Western customs of ceremonial are ones readily associated with worship in other countries and cultures. For example, in Africa and other Eastern countries it is regarded as an insult to God to wear footgear or headgear, while some cultures regard the latter as indispensable. According to Pobee, in some parts of Africa the kiss of peace as a physical kiss would cause offence (though it would in some English congregations too!).

This adaptation of ceremonial was represented in a minor way in the first CSI Prayer Book where in the wedding ceremony provision was made for the giving of a *mangalusutra* rather than a ring. Much more enterprising was the Mass for India of the Bangalore National Liturgical Centre. It is described by Paul Puthanangady as follows: The entrance procession is abandoned and the faithful gather and begin singing devotional songs. When the celebrant enters, he is given a plate of flowers. Water is sprinkled to represent the presence of Christ. The book is garlanded and incensed. The presentation of the bread and wine includes the presentation of a plate with eight flowers. Of the concluding rites, Puthanangady explained:

> It consists of the blessing by the celebrant, expressing the idea of Christian mission with reference to the theme of the Mass. There is no dismissal formula since it is not in accordance with Indian hospitality to send away people after a celebration. The people sing some devotional hymns (*bhajans*) as conclusion of the whole liturgy.[3]

Similar ceremonial changes have been allowed in the recent CSI and Church of North India eucharists. In some African countries there has been more interest in adapting indigenous initiation and funeral customs where these are not explicitly associated with tribal religion.

The question naturally arises as to what other symbolism in worship can be regarded as simply cultural. It has been urged, for example, that in cultures where bread and wine are foreign commodities, these might be replaced by rice or cocoyams, and palm wine. Here we must distinguish between a primary Christian symbolism of the gospels such as baptism in water, and bread and wine for the eucharist, which should in normal circumstances be used, and secondary cultural symbolism such as dress and gestures which change according to time and place.

Architecture and music

Even a limited knowledge of Christian architecture reveals a variety of forms in different lands, from the dome which is the hall-mark of Greek Orthodox churches, to the rock churches of Ethiopia, to wooden Saxon churches, and the great Roman basilicas. Yet after the nineteenth-century 'Gothic revival', the Gothic type was promoted by Europeans as *the* Christian style of church architecture. The Liturgical Movement forced architects and designers to

[3] Paul Puthanangady, 'Liturgical Renewal in India', *Ephemerides Liturgicae*, 91 (1977), pp. 350–66.

think again, and certainly from the 1950s Europe showed signs of escaping from the Gothic style. One concern of the Liturgical Movement was that the decoration and shape of a church building is reflected by what happens inside, but the outside is in one sense of little importance. Thus, Christians in India may wish to build churches in the style of Hindu temples (the influence can be seen on some of the older churches in Kerala belonging to the Indian Syrian communities) and those in rural Africa may wish to take a giant hut as the model.

Likewise with music. It is sometimes forgotten by English-speaking congregations that the organ and robed choir for ordinary parish churches were an innovation of the nineteenth century. But there is no reason why Western styles of ecclesiastical music should be regarded as the only authentic Christian styles of music. The music and melodies of a culture may be pressed into the service of the gospel, and in Africa, for example, the horn, xylophone and drums may be preferable to a harmonium.

Liturgical colours

The so-called 'traditional' five colours for the seasons in the Western church, found in Roman Catholic, Anglican, Lutheran and some Reformed groups, were never standardized until after the Council of Trent in the sixteenth century. Colours do help set the tone for the season because certain colours have particular associations. However, a particular colour does not necessarily have the same significance everywhere. J. S. Pobee pointed out that in many parts of Africa red is associated with sadness and funerals; gold and yellows are festive; blue reflects tenderness and love, and grey is a sign of penance. Black is avoided since it is associated with terror. In India red, for example, is associated with weddings rather than the present Western colour of white. Here then colours may vary from culture to culture to express the appropriate mood.

Rites of passage

The history of marriage and funeral liturgies illustrates just how the Church took over customs and incorporated them into its own evolving liturgies. It has been urged that this should continue to happen in Asia and Africa. The Zaire theologian C. Mubengayi Lwakale proposed that some traditional initiation rites could be included in baptism and confirmation. Among African funeral rites he listed three groups of ceremonies:

1. Practices of no religious significance, e.g. preparing the body.
2. Pagan practices such as consulting a sorcerer.
3. Practices which might be transposed into Christian liturgy such as the taking and removing of mourning garments.

Some Anglican Africans urged the need for liturgy to include reference to the ancestors, which is regarded as fundamental in African culture.[4]

Language and texts

Pobee has pointed out that what African liturgy needs is not translation from a liturgy composed in Latin (or English) for that is a vernacular liturgical face with a Latin soul! What is needed is liturgy composed in the vernacular using the thought-forms of that culture. He suggested that the language of royal courts in African tribes was important for how an African liturgy might address God. The Roman Catholic Church has pioneered a Mass for Zaire, and the Anglican Church in Kenya has also produced its own Kenyan eucharistic liturgy.

One question which quickly arises – as it did in India – is how far it is legitimate to borrow thought-forms which belong not only to another culture, but also to the religions of that culture. The Indian Mass can be criticized for pre-

[4] For instance, H. Sawyerr, *Creative Evangelism*, London, Lutterworth, 1968.

senting Hindu ideas of creation rather than the Judaeo-Christian view, and for also including a reference to the Islamic idea of the inscrutable decrees. Also, the language chosen for this rite was based on classical Sanskrit, which is regarded as esoteric; the CSI and CNI have adopted a lower caste style of language which seems to have been more acceptable.[5]

Western culture and liturgy

It will be apparent that in a good many reports and studies inculturation was regarded as something for the Third World countries, the former 'mission fields'. However, one of the problems of describing the cultures of these countries (apart from isolated communities) is that the traditional cultures are changing as they interact with, or are affected by, Western culture. For better or worse, modernization is linked with industrialization, scientific and medical advances, and new technology, nearly all of which are products of Western culture. But this observation raises also the whole question of just how far modern Western European liturgies can be inculturated, or whether they are in fact already a product of Western culture. This is an extremely difficult question to answer. At one level any modern Western European liturgy must be a product of this culture, compiled by Westerners who have been born and educated and live in this culture. On the other hand this culture is often described as secular, and oriented towards consumerism and agnosticism, and this raises the question of whether these traits have infiltrated liturgical compositions. Ulrich Simon, commenting on the Church of England draft Series 3 Communion Service of 1971, wrote:

[5] K. Virginia Kennerley, 'The use of indigenous sacred literature and theological concepts in Christian Eucharistic Liturgy in India', *Studia Liturgica*, 19 (1989), pp. 143–61; B. D. Spinks, 'The Anaphora for India: Some theological objections to an attempt of inculturation, *Ephemerides Liturgicae*, 96 (1981), pp. 529–49.

> The sociologist will certainly identify this work with the generation from which it has sprung and which it serves. Here is the liturgy of the Western middle class, full of good intentions, decent, and just a little dull. . . . 1971 must be reckoned to be petty bourgeois to the point of nausea.[6]

It is possible to extend this observation to other English liturgical activity in the period 1965–75, and Thaddaeus Schnitker has attempted to find similar correlation in the revision and production of the 1979 *Book of Common Prayer* of the American Episcopal Church.[7] It is easier to see syncretism in 'liturgies for Africa' than in one's own Western liturgies. It may be that only Third World theologians and liturgists can judge fully how far modern Western liturgies have expressed too much the concerns of modern Western culture in place of the gospel.

The failure of the Western Churches to win large masses of what used to be called 'working class people' may indicate a cultural gap in modern liturgies – or more accurately, a subcultural gap. The language which one person finds to be dignified and uplifting tends to be someone else's 'gobbledegook'. Attempts to take seriously the needs of parishes in urban working-class areas are reflected in the Church of England's *Patterns for Worship* (1989), though it is far too early to know whether this will be successful.

H. Richard Neibuhr in his classic study of *Christ and Culture* detected five categories or approaches in Christian theology:

1. Christ against culture, represented by Barth.
2. Christ of culture, where Christianity is absorbed, perhaps represented now by John Hick.
3. Christ above culture – Aquinas.

[6] Ulrich Simon, 'Alternative Services', in SPCK *View Review*, 22, 4 November 1971, pp. 18–19.

[7] B. D. Spinks, 'Christian Worship or Cultural Incantations?', *Studia Liturgica*, 12 (1977), pp. 1–19; T. A. Schnitker, *The Church's Worship*, Berlin, Peter Lang, 1989.

4. Christ and culture in paradox, as in Luther.
5. Christ the transformer of culture.

Geoffrey Wainwright argued that the most promising model is Christ the transformer of culture.[8] According to Moltmann, the Church, and therefore liturgy, is a critical catalyst, bringing indirect infection of a religion or culture by Christian tenets and concepts.[9] Hence if the Arab world of Islam produces a fatalistic attitude, then the encounter with Christianity brings the discovery that the world can be changed. In India it will show through language and concepts that time is not cyclical. And in a Western secular culture it will challenge individualism, and selfish materialism, and dare to speak of the mystery of God and the transcendent. All liturgies in whatever culture will focus on the kingdoms of this world becoming the kingdom of God and his Christ.

Selected Reading

Anscar Chupungo, *Cultural Adaptation of the Liturgy*, New York, Paulist Press, 1982.

— *Liturgies of the Future*, New York, Paulist Press, 1989.

— *Liturgical Inculturation*, Collegeville, Pueblo Liturgical Press, 1992.

David R. Holeton (ed.), *Liturgical Inculturation in the Anglican Communion*, Alcuin/GROW Liturgical Study 15, Bramcote, Grove Books, 1990.

David Power, *Worship, Culture and Theology*, Washington, Pastoral Press, 1990.

Studia Liturgica, 20 (1990) is mainly devoted to this theme.

Philip Tovey, *Inculturation: The Eucharist in Africa*, Alcuin/GROW Liturgical Study 7, Bramcote, Grove Books, 1988.

[8] Geoffrey Wainwright, *Doxology*, London, Epworth Press, 1980.

[9] Jürgen Moltmann, *The Church in the Power of the Spirit*, London, 1977, pp. 152ff.

16
Opposition and Reaction

Almost from its very beginnings the Liturgical Movement has provoked opposition. As late as 1954 Koenker believed its total suppression in the Roman Catholic Church was a real possibility: 'Time and sociological circumstances alone will tell whether in the face of understandable suspicion the movement will gradually gain its objectives or be more and more suppressed.'[1] So violent and deep-felt has the opposition to liturgical reform been that in some Churches it has produced actual schism: among adherents of the late Archbishop Lefebvre and Anglican 'continuing Churches' the loss of the old forms of worship has been a major factor in precipitating the break with the parent Church.

It would be impossible in the scope of this chapter to survey the vast range of arguments that have been raised against the various aspects of the Liturgical Movement throughout the twentieth century. All that can be done is to indicate the broad areas of concern. In many cases, although the specific instances may differ, the fundamental objection is common to both Protestants and Catholics.

A sense of loss

Change in any area of life can be exciting, exhilarating, enjoyable or uncomfortable, painful and dramatic. This is especially true where a person's deepest religious beliefs, feelings and instincts are concerned. Often the whole range

[1] Koenker, *Liturgical Renaissance*, p. 70.

of emotions – positive and negative – can exist alongside each other in a particular individual, congregation or Church. For some, early negative feelings have given way to a more positive evaluation of what has happened. No doubt for others the reverse has been true. It is undeniably the case that the Liturgical Movement has brought bewilderment and a sense of bereavement to many people. Proponents of the movement have not always been as pastorally sensitive as they might have. Central to the experience of many has been the sense of being cut off from their roots. This has been acutely felt among Roman Catholics where the loss of Latin and various forms of personal devotions has cut people off not only from their own childhood but from the experience of Roman Catholics down the centuries and throughout the world. The Latin Mass, for which Catholic martyrs had died, has, it seems to many, been abandoned at a stroke. For Anglicans and others the change has brought the loss of well-known prayers, and for some a loss of identity with the Reformers. In England the wide-scale abandonment of the 1662 *Book of Common Prayer* for the *Alternative Service Book* brought a protest from many outside the Church who believed that an important part of the nation's culture and heritage was under threat.[2] For some the re-ordering of the church building which often accompanied liturgical reform was also painful. Proponents of the changes have argued that it is the occasional attenders who are often the most offended. Regular worshippers are arguably more committed in any case and soon become accustomed to the new rites.

The danger of introversion

Throughout the twentieth century, in much of Europe at least, Church and society have become increasingly less conterminous. Only small proportions of the population of

[2] Martin (ed.), 'Crisis for Cranmer and King James'.

Sweden, England and Spain worship week by week. The reasons for this are complex and range far beyond the question of the Liturgical Movement. It is true, however, that to a large extent the Liturgical Movement has accepted the changed situation and has been concerned to 'get the liturgy right' for the minority that *do* come, without worrying too much about the perceptions and preferences of those who only attend infrequently. Some would argue that this is a regrettable retrenchment, a severing of links with the wider community – the outsider feels even more alienated by the loss of what little familiarity existed. On the other hand, the new rites and styles of worship are 'user friendly' in intention and should be understandable even to the uninitiated. Nevertheless, it is true that the dominant model of 'the Lord's People around the Lord's Table on the Lord's Day' is of a gathered eucharistic community from which the unconfirmed visitor may feel excluded. The answer – to lead such people on to deeper commitment and inclusion – illustrates the crucial relationship between a Church's liturgical life and its evangelistic and pastoral ministry.

Loss of doctrinal purity

Liturgy expresses what Christians believe. To change the liturgy therefore runs the risk of changing doctrine – or at least those doctrines which worshippers regularly hear and absorb and which become part of their Christian identity. The question is further complicated by the fact that liturgies are not timeless documents but reflect the language, thought-forms and priorities of the age in which they were created. Thus, for example, Reformation liturgies tend to contain much about sin and grace, but very little about the Holy Spirit. Sin and grace were crucial issues in the conflicts and debates of the sixteenth century; pneumatology was not. How much of the doctrinal content of a liturgy should be timeless, and how much should it reflect the concerns, insights and context of a particular age and culture?

The question of doctrinal purity often reflects attitudes to the sixteenth-century Reformation in the Western Church. People on both sides of the Catholic/Protestant divide have been inclined to see liturgical reform as the 'corruption' of their Church by 'the other side'. Thus, for example, conservative Roman Catholics have spoken of the creeping Protestantism in the new Mass.[3] Equally, some Protestants have viewed the changes to older models in the shape of the eucharists and the search for common lectionaries as concessions to Rome at the expense of the Reformation heritage.[4]

Clearly, for many such perceptions are influenced by a host of other factors. It is true, of course, that different traditions have taken into their liturgies features which had been characteristic of 'the other side'. Yet, overtly at least, the motivation and process have seldom been of direct borrowing. Rather the changes are a result of going back to a common tradition pre-dating the divide, of which different features have been preserved in different Churches. The general acceptability of such changes is an indication of their rightness, despite the fears of the strongly partisan. Interestingly, both Catholic and Protestant critics are united in their suspicion of a watering-down of the more demanding elements of Christianity in favour of a low-demand liberalism. Both sides would point to the comparative absence from the new rites of contrition and wrath, for example. In places the charge is a fair one. How far is it possible to go in the direction of 'user friendliness' without sacrificing the scandal of particularity and a broad and balanced doctrinal basis?

The place of modern theology

It is not just the doctrinally conservative who are unhappy with the present state of liturgical reform. Much criticism

[3] For instance, M. Davies, *Pope Paul's New Mass*. On page 352 and following he argues that Eucharistic Prayer II, in fact, follows Cranmer.

[4] For instance, Martin and Mullen, *No Alternative*.

has come from liberal and progressive quarters. The Liturgical Movement, it has been claimed, has ignored nearly two hundred years of biblical criticism. Ancient thought-forms and concepts are imported from the Bible directly into the texts of the new rites without any consideration of what critical scholarship has to say about their origin, character and original meaning. For example, passages characterized as 'mythological' are used in the same way as those defined as 'historical'. Some such opposition has focused on the widespread use of 'This is the word of the Lord' to mark the end of Scripture readings. Such a declaration, it is claimed, encourages a credulous fundamentalism, and actually makes faith and worship even harder for the critical explorer.

The creeds, as products of a particular thought-world, also come under attack on the grounds that the categories in which they define the nature of God are alien and irrelevant to the modern world. A parallel criticism is levelled against the assumptions about human nature and society that are encouraged by an uncritical use of biblical imagery and terminology. For some the emphasis in the new rites is simply insufficiently anthropocentric – the transcendent squeezes out the immanent. For others the debate moves into some of the feminist areas touched on in Chapter 14.

A weakness of such criticism has often been the failure to provide an alternative set of concepts to replace the biblical ones. Unless and until an alternative system of imagery could be agreed – which itself seems highly unlikely – it is difficult to see how liturgies can do other than draw their primary (and secondary) thought-forms and concepts from the Bible.

Antiquarianism

If the Liturgical Movement has been attacked for not being radical enough by liberal theologians, it has also faced the same accusation from circles usually thought of as much more conservative. Part of the Liturgical Movement's aim is to go back to the sources, to the ancient common tradition. What sources could be more ancient or universal, it is claimed, than the worship described in the New Testament itself? For some, such a perspective has been reinforced by an experience of the Charismatic Movement which has brought a sense of immediacy and identity with the New Testament Church. The rapid growth of the House Church Movement in many places is in part due to a desire to recreate the 'pure' worship of the New Testament, freed from the accretions of the centuries. For many such Christians the historical concerns of the Liturgical Movement are irrelevant.

A closely allied concern has been expressed in another way. Why has the Liturgical Movement 'stopped the clock' at the third and fourth centuries? Hippolytus was at best an anti-Pope and his liturgy did not become normative in the Roman Church; why then is his eucharistic prayer so widely adopted as the model in many parts of the Liturgical Movement? Similarly, why is the full-blown fourth-century West Syrian anaphora followed so slavishly in many modern compositions? Is the Liturgical Movement not guilty of 'patristic fundamentalism'?[5] Even so eminent a liturgist as the late Geoffrey Cuming questioned the West Syrian model and wondered whether a series of short variable prayers might not be preferable.[6] The choice of third- and fourth-century models can, of course, be defended, but the criticism concerning their dominance in the Liturgical Movement to date is an important one. Already there are experiments with less traditionally structured eucharistic prayers.[7]

[5] Bradshaw, 'The Liturgical Use and Abuse of Patristics'.

[6] G. J. Cuming, 'Four Very Early Anaphoras', in *Worship*, 58 (1984), pp. 168–72.

[7] For instance, the suggestions of the Liturgical Commission of the Church of England in the report *Patterns for Worship* (1989).

The loss of the transcendent

Liturgy should enable an encounter with God. Clearly, such a personal experience will vary from one occasion to another, from one individual to another and from one congregation to another. Yet, even accepting the necessary unpredictable element in such an encounter, it is true that for some the new rites and the method of their enactment have made it harder to approach God. For some the very text has become empty, cerebral and desacralized. Poetic, evocative and awe-inspiring language has been replaced by flat bourgeois phrases. Everything has been reduced to the lowest common denominator. The obsession with intelligibility has driven out the glory, mystery and holiness. Similar accusations are levelled at the way the rite is performed. The drama where heaven and earth meet has been replaced by the dynamics of a committee meeting with hymns. The westward celebration of the eucharist creates a closed human circle from which God is excluded. Those attending now expect to be entertained, and their commitment held with constant novelty. Features such as liturgical dance smack of sensuality and exhibitionism. The accusation of indulgent man-centredness is often made.

Such perspectives often focus on church music. The displacement of the organ as the sole musical instrument in most of the Western Churches and its replacement by guitars and keyboards – the instruments of 'pop' music – has aroused much controversy and opposition. At the heart of many such issues is the relationship between worship and culture. In much of the world the latter is in transition, sometimes of a rapid nature. To what extent should worship relate to and follow it?

Clearly the reactions to the Liturgical Movement are part of the developments and shifts taking part in the World Church throughout the twentieth century and it is impossible to explore them all. How the movement itself is responding to such criticisms is difficult to quantify. There are parts of the Church where they would be seen as irrelevant and worship patterns continue to evolve further and further from traditional roots. Conversely, there are signs that a sense of loss of the transcendent and the need for a more positive assessment of continuity are being taken seriously in some quarters. Liturgical material published in the last decade or so is often less bare than that produced in the 1960s and 1970s.[8] Whether the twenty-first century will produce a substantial reaction remains to be seen.

Selected Reading

P. Bradshaw, 'The Liturgical Use and Abuse of Patristics', in K. Stevenson (ed.), *Liturgy Reshaped*, London, SPCK, 1982.

M. Davies, *Pope Paul's New Mass*, Chawleigh, Augustine Publishing, 1981.

W. J. Grisbrooke, 'Liturgical Reform and Liturgical Renewal', in *Studia Liturgica*, 21 (1991).

D. Martin (ed.), 'Crisis for Cranmer and King James', in *PN Review*, 13, 6, 1979.

— and P. Mullen (eds), *No Alternative: The Prayer Book Controversy*, Oxford, Basil Blackwell, 1981.

B. Morris (ed.), *Ritual Murder: Essays on Liturgical Reform*, Manchester, Carcanet Press, 1980.

[8] For instance, *Lent, Holy Week and Easter*, produced by the Liturgical Commission of the Church of England in 1986.

17

The Daily Office, Pastoral Offices and Ordination: Highlights and Questions

The Daily Office

One of the problems with the Daily Office or Divine Office is that it is not common to all traditions, and the number of services which make up the Office also differs. The Roman Catholic Church had maintained the eight offices of the Breviary (Matins, Lauds, Prime, Terce, Sext, None, Vespers and Compline) which had undergone only slight modifications and changes in the centuries following the Council of Trent. Central to the Offices, which were in most places recited privately by the clergy, was the recitation of the Psalter in the course of a week. The Anglican tradition had reduced the Offices to two, Morning and Evening Prayer. Cranmer had spread the Psalter over a month, and had made Scripture readings from the Old and New Testaments another central feature of the Offices. The Wesleyan Methodists had inherited this tradition, though the 1936 *Book of Offices* contained only a version of Morning Prayer. The Reformed tradition had abandoned the Office with all set forms of liturgy, but the liturgies of Hunter and Orchard had provided Sunday Morning and Evening Services which were inspired by the structure and contents of the Anglican forms. Also, Dr Nathaniel Micklem prepared a collection of Morning and Evening devotions in *Prayers and Praises* (1941), which proved popular among Free Church ministers as a daily devotion.

A number of questions were posed by the Liturgical Movement concerning the Daily Office: How many services should there be? Eight services were derived from the monastic discipline, but should this number of services each day apply also to secular clergy? And what about the laity? The Roman Catholic tradition had reduced the Office to a discipline for clergy and religious orders, but historically some Offices were for the whole Church. How could they be made suitable for lay participation? In the Anglican tradition the week-day Offices tended to be a discipline for the clergy, but then forming one or both of the forms of congregational worship on Sundays as Matins and Choral Evensong. But should they have more variations? And should they be made suitable for the more devout laity?

The new Roman Catholic reforms abolished Prime as an Office. Lauds and Vespers became the chief hours, and as Morning and Evening Prayer have been issued separately for use by the laity, and in places these have proved popular. Sunday Vespers has slowly started to replace Rosary and Benediction. Matins becomes a 'reading office' and can be said at any time. In religious houses Terce, Sext and None are retained, but when recited elsewhere only one need be recited, corresponding most nearly to the time of day. Compline was revised to make it a fitting close for the day.

There is a rich variety of canticles and hymns in these new Offices, though the Psalter, now spread over four weeks, is still recited in course. Only short Scripture readings are provided, allowing meditation. There is still lack of clarity as for whom the Daily Office is intended, it still being mainly a provision for the clergy.

In England the JLG published a Daily Office in 1969, revised in 1978. The Baptist liturgist, Stephen Winward, wrote an introductory essay, arguing that the Office was something between public worship and private prayer, representing the continual sacrifice of praise offered by the Church, and the individual could simply tune in and make his or her contribution. (This was, in fact, a new definition of the Office.) He also argued that the twin pillars of the Office are the recitation of the Psalter and Scripture reading. The actual provisions were for the morning and evening, Monday to Saturday, with a Psalter spread over thirteen weeks, a lectionary providing three lessons (two in the morning, one in the evening), collects, a variety of canticles, intercessions and thanksgivings.

These forms were adopted by the Methodist Sacramental Fellowship (for ministers), and they also influenced the Church of England revisions in the 1980 ASB. These latter were rather tame revisions, and left most of Cranmer intact but in modern English. Variations were mainly for weekday recitation.

More recent research into the origins and development of the Daily Office has suggested that these revisions outlined above are unsatisfactory. To begin with it is far from certain as to whether common daily prayer was originally only morning and evening, or whether it was three times a day. What is more certain is that there was a difference between what is called the 'cathedral' Office, which was presided over by secular clergy and celebrated with a lay congregation, and the 'monastic' Office, which was an individual devotional exercise of monks, though it could be corporate. In the 'cathedral' form the service centred upon praise and intercession, not Bible reading with exposition (even today the East Syrian Daily Office has no Scripture readings); neither was the Psalter recited in course, but certain fixed psalms were selected as appropriate for the time of day. Hymns and canticles were prominent in this corporate act of worship. The Evening Office made particular use of the symbol of light, and later, in nearly all traditions, the use of incense in association with Psalm 141, which was appropriate for an evening service. This was the *lucernarium*. The 'monastic' Office, by contrast, was based upon the recitation of the Psalter and reading of Scripture as an individual spiritual and devotional exercise. In the course of time, particularly as bishops were appointed from monasteries, the 'monastic' form made a large impact on the 'cathedral' form, and it is thus that a tradition has emerged where the Psalter (and subsequently for the Reformers, the Bible readings) seems to be the main pillar of the Office.

The American *Lutheran Book of Worship* 1978 and *Lutheran Worship* 1982, and the Anglican Canadian Book of 1984 make provision for *lucernarium*, and an evening service that is more flexible, and centres upon praise and intercession. There is much more variety. More recent still, the English Anglican Franciscan Office, *Celebrating Common Prayer* (1992) represents the combination of the best ideas from recent revisions in various Churches, together with the insights of recent research on the origin of the Office. The structure is basically praise and intercession, with a great variety of canticles and responsorial material, hymnody, and selected psalmody rather than psalmody in course. It also provides for *lucernarium*, and other optional symbolism in the Office. It may be congregational or individual. Provision for the celebration of *lucernarium* has also been developed in the Roman Catholic Church.

Marriage

Marriage ceremonies differ quite considerably between the Eastern and Western traditions. Whereas the former are full of nuptial imagery, and regard the couple as royal lovers celebrating marriage in the presence of God, the Western tradition has been more concerned to effect a validly contracted marriage. The older Western forms were mainly two-fold: either nuptial blessing within the Mass, celebrated in church, or blessing of the rings and the bridal chamber in the home. The domestic consent gradually passed over to the church, and the whole ceremony took place before the door of the church before entering the church for the Nuptial Mass. The Catholic reforms made by the Council of Trent gave a bare minimum for effecting a valid Catholic marriage, and some churches simply used this bare minimum. In marriages with a non-Catholic partner this was all that was allowed. A Catholic couple could have a full Nuptial Mass after the preliminary consent, exchange of vows and blessing of the ring. The Anglican reforms from 1549 to 1662 show an evolution where the whole ceremony took place in the church, but the preliminary consent and exchange of vows and giving of the ring is expanded with a long exhortation and prayers, and a communion is only recommended; in reality the latter fell into disuse, and no propers were provided for it. The result in the Anglican tradition was the creation of an 'Occasional Office' by the expansion of what had been originally the legal preliminaries. Most Free Church rites have tended to follow a modified version of the Anglican structure.

In 1969 the new Roman rite for marriage was promulgated. Now the legal consent, exchange of vows and giving of the ring were no longer a preliminary to the Nuptial Mass, but were to be celebrated within the Liturgy of the Word, and the Nuptial Blessing could be given outside the Mass. This is a much more satisfactory arrangement. Three new Nuptial Blessings were also given. Permission remained for local and national variation and custom, but in 1969 the English Church chose not to develop this option. At present a new revision is being prepared for England and Wales which takes advantage of this provision. It proposes 'staged' rites, with prayers for the engagement and for anniversaries, as well as an expansion of the marriage service with a role for the families of the bride and groom, and the inclusion of the popular ceremony of the 'wedding candle'.[1]

The Church of England revised rite in the late 1980 ASB allows the service to take the form of the Liturgy of the Word, or retain its 1662 shape, though there is now provision for propers for a Nuptial Communion. It allows for the

[1] *Liturgy*, 10.5 (1986): C. Walsh, 'Revising the Rites of Marriage', *Priests and People*, 6:7 (1992).

blessing of ring(s), and is more celebratory in character than the older form. The introductory exhortation is retained, but completely modernized. The Methodist 1975 rite follows the Liturgy of the Word pattern, with considerable enrichment in terms of the prayers, and allows for the possibility of a communion. The URC 1980 and 1989 rites still follow the older 'occasional service' pattern, with Scripture readings after the actual marriage ceremony, though the 1989 rite does mention the possibility of a communion service.

In the English revisions one can detect a move towards setting the legal side (still the main concern in the West) in terms of consent and vows within a Liturgy of the Word, and the reintroduction of provision for a communion service. The new proposals for the English Roman Catholic rite may well force the other Churches to enrich their rites, particularly perhaps with the use of the 'wedding candle'. In comparison with the Eastern rites, there is still too much emphasis on establishing a legal contract rather than with celebrating a marriage in God's presence. Nor has the ecclesial setting of marriage yet been satisfactorily resolved.

Funeral rites

Most classical Christian burial rites have a five-stage ritual: At the house when the body is washed and anointed; psalms and liturgical chants during a procession to the church; the service in church (in the West a Mass); procession to the place of burial; the act of committal at the grave. In the medieval Western service there is a shift towards prayer in the presence of the body, with concern for sin and judgement. The 1614 *Rituale Romanum* reduced some of the medieval excesses, though it still catered for the five-stage ceremony.[2] The Anglican Prayer Book reduced the five-stage structure, and by 1552 there was no longer provision for a

[2] Rowell, *Christian Burial*.

Mass or psalmody, though the latter was restored in 1662. While less gloomy than the medieval Catholic rites, the Protestant reaction to purgatory meant that little of the service is concerned with the departed person. Later Methodist and Congregationalist rites tended to follow the Prayer Book pattern of service.

Revision of the funeral services in the latter part of the twentieth century has taken place in an atmosphere where death is hastily removed from the land of the living. The five-stage ceremony is rendered obsolete since most dead bodies in the urban West are removed to a mortuary, and then brought to the church, or more commonly, the crematorium, by motorized transport. The new Roman rite still allows for a five-stage rite where it is practical, but the rite can be adopted to local custom. It provides for a three-stage rite: vigil in the home, the Mass with commendation and farewell, and the burial. The gloom of the old rite is transformed by confident thanksgiving.

The Church of England ASB rite takes the form of the Liturgy of the Word with committal, with provision for a eucharist. There is also a short service for the bringing of the body into the church, though nothing is provided specifically for use in the home. It is not generally the custom of the Methodist and URC to have a eucharist; both Churches present a service similar to the Anglican one (though by no means a copy), namely a Liturgy of the Word structure. The URC rite provides for a service in the home.

The provision in the Roman Catholic and URC rites for prayer in the home when a death has occurred is a welcome attack on the increasingly Western urban tendency to remove a dead body from the presence of the living as quickly as possible. The new rites generally are marked by a desire to proclaim the paschal truth of Christianity, and introduce praise rather than sorrow in the face of death. For example, the Methodist 1975 rite contains a special thanksgiving prayer proclaiming the resurrection, and the Anglican and the URC rites of 1980 and 1989 contain the *Te*

Deum. However, the non-Roman rites still have a problem as regards speaking about the departed person. There is an unresolved tension between the implications of justification by faith and baptism on the one hand, and fear of medieval bargaining for the dead. The rites seem more for the mourners (a source of comfort and consolation) rather than an expression of eschatology for a departed member of the Church of God. Part of the problem, particularly where there is an established or majority Church, is that a church funeral is still the choice made by most families even though they, and the departed, may have had no church connection. The departed may have been good, bad, indifferent, but probably not a member of an ecclesial group. There are dangers of appearing to teach universalism and too much might be claimed for the departed person. Yet to say nothing other than what the Anglican rite appears to say – 'we believe in the resurrection, and hope he/she did too' – is to negate eschatology and ecclesiology. Baptism and faith (however weak) count for something; and as the Church gathers to accompany a body of one created in the image of God to its resting place, prayers proclaiming this passing over seem appropriate. Belief in the unity of God's Church on earth and in heaven would seem not to rule out some form of prayers for the departed in the sense that they are still part of God's Church. Perhaps Protestant rites need to have the courage of their soteriology!

From 1993 the Church of England Liturgical Commission has started to think of revision of the 1980 ASB rite, and is considering an anthology of prayers from which the minister can select those most appropriate for the particular individual and family.

Ordination

The Roman Catholic rites found in the *Pontificale Romanum* of 1595, and revised slightly in 1645, represented a standardization of the variant texts of medieval Pontificals.

The Pontifical was the bishop's private book and, in the days of manuscript, a bishop would write in and add his own peculiar liturgical fancies. The Pontifical distinguished between the major and minor orders. The former consisted of bishop, priest (presbyter) and deacon, together with the subdeacon, though the status of the latter had varied. The minor orders were acolyte, reader, exorcist and door-keeper. Most of the ceremonies including the delivery of suitable tools or symbols of office, but only bishop, priest and deacon including the laying on of hands. The rites had had a complicated history and were the result of combining the old Roman rites with those of the Gallican rite – in effect, a double ordination.[3] Candidates for the priesthood had to graduate through the minor orders.

The Anglican rite had reduced the orders to three – bishop, priest and deacon, and Cranmer had drawn up his rites by combining elements of the medieval Sarum rite with the rite drawn up by Martin Bucer. Wesley had retained this three-fold ministry for his American Abridgement, but on the authority of Edward Stillingfleet and Peter King, he was convinced that presbyters had the right to ordain, and though his 1786 English Abridgement contained rites of superintendents, elders and deacons, only that for elders or ministers was used. The Reformed tradition had a complicated ecclesiology in theory, but in practice the minister was the sole order. In Presbyterianism he was ordained by fellow presbyters whereas in early Congregationalism he was ordained by the congregation. Later Congregationalism incorporated the Presbyterian method.

The main debate in the ecumenical age has been the validity of ministries. On the one hand Anglicans have defended the validity of their three-fold orders against the official papal declaration of invalidity of 1896; on the other

[3] P. de Puniet, *The Roman Pontifical*, ET 1932; C. Vogel, *Medieval Liturgy. An Introduction to the Sources*, Washington, Pastoral Press, 1986.

hand Anglicans were suspicious of all non-episcopal ministries, and have tried to persuade the Free Churches to adopt the three-fold pattern.

In the revised rites, the Roman Church simplified the rites, and these stress the pastoral rather than juridical role of ministry. The orders of exorcist, door-keeper and subdeacon have been abolished. As regards the major orders, it is made clear that ordination consists of the laying on of hands and prayer, which includes an epicletic petition relating to the gifts of the particular office being bestowed. The symbolism of instruments is retained, but is simplified, and anointing is also retained. The *Apostolic Tradition* attributed to Hippolytus has been influential in this revision, and in the ordination of a bishop the prayer has been taken over from the *Apostolic Tradition* with only a few minor editorial changes.

Throughout the Anglican Communion revision of the existing ordinals has been undertaken, drawing particularly on the ordinal drawn up for South India. The validity of the actual rite has been regarded as unquestionable. The rite has also indirectly affected revision in the Methodist Church.

Although there is still an obvious difference between provision for episcopal Churches and those where there is a single ordained ministry, there is remarkable consensus in liturgical terms of what ordination entails. The congregation is given a role, as they had in the ancient rites, expressing that this is the concern of the whole Church of God. The act of ordination itself is regarded as being performed by a duly qualified and recognized president (bishop or superintendent) and is by laying on of hands with prayer. Some Anglican rites allow for anointing and the delivery of suitable instruments of office. Most Protestant rites include the giving of a Bible, and some include the giving of the right hand of fellowship. On the whole, the tensions which surround ordination are not liturgical questions so much as ecumenical and doctrinal questions, such as the recognition of different ministries between

Churches, what constitutes apostolic succession, the ordination of women and, where episcopacy is given high regard, the awkward status of suffragan and assistant bishops. These are questions beyond the liturgical rites.

Selected Reading

P. F. Bradshaw, *Ordination Rites of theAncient Churches of East and West*, New York, Pueblo, 1990.

Paul Bradshaw, 'Daily Prayer' in K. W. Stevenson and B. D. Spinks (eds), *The Identity of Anglican Worship*, London, Mowbray, 1991, pp. 69–79.

J. Douglas Davies, *Cremation Today and Tomorrow*, Alcuin/GROW Liturgical Study 16, Bramcote, Grove Books, 1990.

George Guiver, *Company of Voices*, London, SPCK, 1988.

J. Mullett, *One People, One Church, One Song*, London, Hodder & Stoughton, 1968.

Geoffrey Rowell, *The Liturgy of Christian Burial*, London, Alcuin Club/SPCK, 1977.

Richard Rutherford, *The Death of a Christian: The Rite of Funerals*, New York, Pueblo, 1980.

D. Stancliffe, et al. (eds), *Something Understood*, London, Hodder & Stoughton, 1993.

K. W. Stevenson, *Nuptial Blessing*, London, Alcuin Club/SPCK, 1982.

—*To Join Together, The Rite of Marriage*, New York, Pueblo, 1987.

Robert Taft, *The Liturgy of the Hours in East and West*, Collegeville, Liturgical Press, 1986.

W. Vos and G. Wainwright (eds), *Ordination Rites. Past and Present*. Papers Read at the 1979 Congress of Societas Liturgica, Rotterdam 1979 (= *Studia Liturgica*, 13 [1979]).

18
Snapshots of the Movement in North America

In terms of the Liturgical Movement, the Churches of North America mirrored their European counterparts, and the events and rites which have been described for Europe and the United Kingdom all have parallels, though with their own American character.

The Roman Catholic Church

In the United States the dissemination of the Liturgical Movement as pioneered by Beauduin, Herwegen and Parsch was initially centred at St John's Abbey, Collegeville, Minnesota, in the hands of Dom Virgil Michel (1890–1938). Between February 1924 and August 1925 Michel visited several Benedictine centres in Europe, including Mont César and Maria Laach. He became imbued with the Liturgical Movement's concern for intelligible liturgy and its commitment to social justice. On his return he persuaded his Abbot, Alcuin Deutsch, to allow him to embark on a programme to harness the energies of St John's Abbey to the goal of liturgical awakening in America as Beauduin had done at Mont César. To this end in 1926 he organized two projects. The first was the journal *Orate Fratres* (subsequently called *Worship*) which first appeared in November 1926, and which became the organ of the American Liturgical Movement. Its aim was the 'wider spread of the true understanding of, and participation in, the Church's worship by the general laity in order to foster the corporate life of the natural social units of the Church – the parishes'.[1] The second project was the founding of the Liturgical Press which, among other works, published English translations of the writings of the European pioneers of the movement. Michel's own contributions illustrated his varied commitments to lay participation, social justice and, by 1933, vernacular in the liturgy.

Orate Fratres was published at St John's under the editorship of Michel. Two other names are associated with the birth of the journal – Martin Hellreigel (1891–1981) and Gerald Ellard (1894–1963). Hellreigel was very much a pastoral practitioner, and had introduced the Dialogue Mass at the convent where he was chaplain. His pastoral teaching at the convent was reproduced in a parish setting in St. Louis. Ellard by contrast was more of a scholar, and during his studies in Europe became acquainted with Herwegen, Parsch and Jungmann. From 1932 he taught liturgy in Kansas. Among his publications are *Men at Work and Worship: America Joins the Liturgical Movement* (1940), and *The Mass in Transition* (1955).

Virgil Michel's early death in 1938 created a vacuum at St John's which was quickly filled by Dom Godfrey Diekmann (1909–). Diekmann's own studies had been centred on Tertullian, but he had also stayed at Maria Laach and had 'caught' the atmosphere of Casel and Herwegen. Diekmann took over and developed *Orate Fratres*, and gathered a team of regular contributors, including H. A. Reinhold and Frederick McManus. He took a leading part in instituting Liturgical Weeks and Liturgical Conferences. He became a regular participant in the International Liturgical Conferences, and was later to serve as a consultant to the Pontifical Liturgical Preparatory Commission of Vatican II, arguing very strongly for the vernacular. Although passed over for the first session of Vatican II, he was appointed a *peritus*

[1] *Orate Fratres*, 3 (1929), p. 186.

(scholars who offered advice and expertise to the Council) for the second session. He was also a founder member of the International Committee for English in the Liturgy (ICEL).

The movement was not welcomed by all Catholic groups in America, and its advocates were regarded with suspicion in some quarters. Diekmann himself was at one stage barred from being a visiting professor at the Catholic University of Washington. Another advocate, H. W. Reinhold, fell foul of his bishop in the Yakima diocese, and the Bishop of St. Cloud persuaded Diekmann to cease publishing Reinhold's contributions in *Worship*. Reinhold found refuge in another diocese, and went on to write a number of influential books, including *Bringing the Mass to the People* (1960), and *The Dynamics of the Liturgy* (1961).

Frederick McManus (1923–), a professor of canon law at the Catholic University of Washington, has also been an influential figure in the American Catholic movement. His doctorate was on the history of the Congregation of Sacred Rites which was established in 1588. He became a leading commentator on the revised rites for Holy Week, and a regular contributor to *Worship*. Along with Diekmann he served as a consultant to the Pontifical Liturgical Commission, and served as a *peritus* from the first session. He too, took a leading role in ICEL.

The journal *Worship*, already an international journal as *Orates Fratres* in 1929, continues to be the journal spearheading liturgical thought in the USA. The fact that ICEL has its headquarters at Washington has further ensured that American Catholicism is in the forefront of developing the new liturgies, and 'Englishing' them.

The Episcopal Church

The Episcopal Church had revised its *Book of Common Prayer* in 1928. The Standing Liturgical Commission (SLC) was set up as a successor to the 1928 Revision Committee. In

1943 it proposed that the General Convention authorize them to present a draft revision in 1949. This was refused, but in 1946 the Convention did authorize the SLC to produce a series of Prayer Book Studies, of essays and experimental texts and schemes, the first appearing in 1950. The series was to extend over the next twenty-five years, resulting in a new Prayer Book.

Revived interest in liturgical origins and scholarship were evident in Edward L. Parsons and Bayard H. Jones, *The American Prayer Book: Its origins and Principles* (1937). The insights of the continental Liturgical Movement were developed by W. P. Ladd, and may be seen in his *Prayer Book Interleaves* (1942). However, more significant was the founding of the Associated Parishes (akin to Parish and People), incorporated in November 1946 by John Patterson, John Keene, Samuel West and Massey Shepherd Jr. Of these names, that of Massey Shepherd Jr was to figure prominently not only in spreading the insights of the movement, but also in scholarship, teaching, and in the Prayer Book Studies leading to revision. (Shepherd was vice-chairman of the SLC from 1964 to 1976, an Anglican observer as the third session of Vatican II, and appointed to the Consilium for the Implementation of the Constitution on the Sacred Liturgy). Associated Parishes published tracts devoted to explaining the theology and use of the 1928 American *Book of Common Prayer*. In 1958 it held a conference, and the papers were published as *The Liturgical Renewal of the Church* (1961); a further conference of 1959 produced *The Eucharist and Liturgical Renewal* (1960). By 1962 Associated Parishes was pushing for liturgical revision rather more radical than a light revision of 1928, and since it had strong representation on the SLC, the result was *Prayer Book Studies XVII: The Liturgy of the Lord's Supper* (1966). In 1970 a radical proposal on initiation was set out in *Prayer Book Studies XVIII*, which together with *Prayer Book Studies 19–24* (also 1970), made up 'Services for Trial Use', or the 'Green Book'. Further revision resulted in the Draft Book, succeeded by the Proposed Book, which in 1979 became the official liturgy of the Episcopal Church. Urban Holmes has described as follows:

> The new prayer book has, consciously or unconsciously, come to emphasize that understanding of the Christian experience which one might describe as a postcritical apprehension of symbolic reality and life in the community. It is consonant with Ricoeur's 'second naivete' and is more expressive of Husserl, Heidegger, Otto, and Rahner than Barth or Brunner. It embraces a Logos Christology. This viewpoint was shaped liturgically at Maria Laach, transmitted to Anglicanism by Herbert, Ladd and Shepherd, and reinforced by Vatican II and a cluster of theologians and teachers who are, directly or indirectly, part of the theological movement reflected in that most significant gathering of the church in the twentieth century.[2]

Among the scholars and teachers in the Episcopal Church, names such as Massey Shepherd Jr, Boone Porter, Thomas Talley, Marion Hatchett, Leonel Mitchell and Louis Weil stand out.

The Lutheran Church

There were several separate Lutheran groups in the USA originating from different ethnic or language groups, or internal Lutheran disputes. Many of these had amalgamated, and most now form one Church, the Evangelical Lutheran Church of America. In 1966 the main groups were the Lutheran Church of America, the American Lutheran Church, the Evangelical Lutheran Church and the Lutheran Church – Missouri Synod. These, together with the Evangelical Lutheran Church of Canada, joined in an Inter-Lutheran Commission on worship in an attempt to produce a common liturgy. Between 1969 and 1975 the Commission produced a series of new services issued as *Contemporary*

[2] Urban T. Holmes, 'Education for Liturgy: an Unfinished Symphony in Four Movements', in Burson (ed.), *Worship Points the Way*, p. 137.

Worship. After experiment and debate these were brought together in the *Lutheran Book of Worship* (1978). One of the main compilers of this work was Eugene Brand.

The Inter-Lutheran Commission on Worship had been set up at the instigation of the conservative Lutheran Church – Missouri Synod. Ironically this Church felt that the 1978 book had made too many departures from traditional Lutheran liturgy and doctrine in a Rome-ward direction. As a result this body brought out its emended edition of the 1978 book under the title *Lutheran Worship* (1982). Among those involved in this latter was Professor Norman Nagel of Concordia Seminary, St. Louis, who wrote the preface.

Both books show the influence of the Liturgical Movement, but *Lutheran Worship* is more conscious of adhering to classical Lutheran forms and, for example, is more reluctant to adopt eucharistic prayers resembling the classic pattern of the fourth and fifth centuries.

The Reformed Tradition

Presbyterians

The Presbyterian Churches in the USA (major reunions took place in 1958 and 1983) have a complex background, the Dutch Reformed Church being one major source of influence. In 1906 the General Assembly of the Presbyterian Church in the USA issued a *Book of Common Worship* which was revised in 1932 and again in 1946. A Joint Committee on Worship of the Presbyterian Church in the USA and the United Presbyterian Church in the USA produced a Directory for Worship in 1961. In 1964 a leaflet service for the Lord's Day was issued which included a two-year lectionary. In 1966 *The Book of Common Worship* was published which was a book of provisional services. In 1970 the Presbyterian Church in the USA and the Cumberland Presbyterian Church produced the *Worshipbook* in 1970, and in 1972 a *Worshipbook* which combined services and hymns. The impact of the Liturgical Movement was evident in that the main service envisaged in the *Worshipbook* was the eucharist. The book also contained a modified version of the Roman Catholic triennial lectionary. Problems of inclusive language resulted in suggested emendations which were published in the quarterly *Reformed Liturgy and Music*, and the Advisory Council on Discipleship and Worship produced a pamphlet version of the eucharistic liturgy from the *Worshipbook*, revised to use inclusive language. In 1980 the process of developing a new book of services began, and in 1983 a draft was issued for use and comment; the final rites appeared as *Book of Common Worship* in 1993.

Much of the editorship of the *Worshipbook* was in the hands of David G. Buttrick. Other notable American Presbyterian liturgists include Horace T. Allen Jr, J. M. Maxwell and Craig Douglas Erickson.

United Church of Christ

This Church brought together former Congregationalist Churches, Evangelical Churches, and the German Reformed congregations. Apart from the latter, whose denomination had produced the famous Mercersburg Liturgy in the nineteenth century, most of these Churches had no real liturgical tradition, though individual churches and ministers did produce liturgies. It was a new departure when the Church produced 'denomination' liturgies in the 1960s: The Lord's Day Service (1964), Services of Word and Sacrament (1966), both of which were published in 1969 as *Services of the Church*. In 1970 a new Lectionary based upon the Roman Catholic Lectionary was issued, and in 1976 the *Book of Worship: The United Church of Christ* was published.

The United Methodist Church

A new Hymnal and *Book of Worship* were published in the early 1960s, before the denomination had really taken on board the implications of the Liturgical Movement and the changes which came from Vatican II. In the 1970s a variety of texts were published, the main revisions being printed as *Supplemental Worship Resources*, resulting in seventeen such booklets. Writing in 1981, James White, one of the chief drafters, said: 'With the United Methodist Church currently the only major denomination left in the field of liturgical revision, there is evidence some congregations in other denominations are using SWR materials in place of or in addition to their own.'[3] Indeed, 'second generation' revisions of the five basic services (Word, Table, Baptism, Marriage, Funerals) appeared in 1980 in *We Gather Together*, and a further stage of revision is found in *The Book of Services* (1985), and a final version in *The United Methodist Hymnal* (1989).

These snapshots have been concerned with the USA, but a similar tale can be told for Canada, with the Roman Catholic Church, Church of Canada (Anglican) and United Church of Canada. The cumulative material serves to underline the widespread adoption of the insights of the Liturgical Movement.

Selected Reading

Malcolm C. Burson, *Worship Points the Way*, New York, Seabury Press, 1981.

R. W. Franklin and Robert L. Spaeth, *Virgil Michel, American Catholic*, Collegeville, The Liturgical Press, 1988.

Kathleen Hughes, *The Monk's Tale. A Biography of Godfrey Diekmann OSB*, Collegeville, The Liturgical Press, 1991.

Robert L. Tuzik (comp.), *How Firm a Foundation: Leaders of the Liturgical Movement*, Chicago, Liturgy Training Publications, 1990.

James F. White, *Christian Worship in Transition*, Nashville, Abingdon, 1976.

— *Protestant Worship. Traditions in Transition*, Louisville, Kentucky, Westminster/John Knox Press, 1989.

[3] James White, 'Towards a Liturgical Strategy', in Burson, op. cit., p. 148.

19

Where Next?

The Liturgical Movement

> seeks a rediscovery of those norms of liturgical worship of the Bible and the early Church which lie behind Reformation divisions and medieval distortions, and which are fundamental to Christian liturgy in every time and place. It aims, however, not at an attempt to resuscitate the liturgy of the early Church in the twentieth century, but at the restatement of the fundamentals in forms and expressions which can enable the liturgy to be the living prayer and work of the church today.[1]

The above definition suggests that the day may come when the Liturgical Movement has achieved its aims: when the ancient norms and fundamentals have been rediscovered and restated in contemporary expression. However, as many of the preceding chapters have suggested, the likelihood of such a day dawning seems increasingly remote. Indeed, the very concept of 'arriving' at all would be repudiated by many. One of the most lasting legacies of the twentieth century, so far as the Church is concerned, is the expectation of continuous change. A dominant motif has been of the Church as a *pilgrim* people – a people in transit, who will not arrive at their destination until the Parousia. Such a framework creates an atmosphere of provisionality – everything is potentially temporary, the permanent has not yet been attained. This is reflected in all areas of Church life: for example, doctrinal definitions (such as the creeds)

[1] J. C. Davies, *A New Dictionary of Liturgy and Worship*, p. 314.

are seen as belonging to a particular period and not necessarily having the same authority in periods which use different thought-forms. From certain perspectives it can appear that the Christian faith itself is undergoing a process of redefinition – a process which some would want to hasten, and others to resist strenuously. Liturgical revision is clearly a major way in which change becomes manifest. An acceptance of 'inclusive language', for example, leads to the liturgical texts being re-written. Furthermore, many Churches became accustomed to a rapid succession of texts in the 1960s and 1970s, and there is an expectation that the succession will continue. For some Churches it appears that only economic factors have stemmed the flow.

The liturgical forms produced in the middle of the second half of the century (the period which Davies called 'the harvest time of liturgical revision') bore a strong family likeness.[2] There are signs that that likeness is now under threat. As has been shown, the patristic norms have recently been themselves challenged. Further, the issue of indigenization undermines to a substantial extent any concept of uniformity. Claims to freedom and creativity in the Spirit erode it still further. The demand not only for liturgies for special occasions, but also for special groups, such as feminist liturgies, gay liturgies, youth liturgies and so on, calls in question the catholic nature of worship. One possible scenario for the future of liturgical reform, therefore, is a sudden centrifugal outburst, resulting in a kaleidoscope of patterns and forms both between and within Churches.

Other scenarios are possible. In 1985 Davies warned that 'the contemporary scene is witnessing a recrudescence of a conservatism that could well impede further liturgical experimentation and even blur the impact of what has been achieved'.[3] Not all Christians are excited by continual

[2] Ibid., p. v.

[3] Ibid., p. vi. Davies himself regretted this, maintaining that worship should be 'liberating and challenging, and therefore is not the undercurrent of resistance to change to be itself resisted . . . ?'

change and there is a real desire for the Church and its worship to exhibit stability in a highly unstable world. In secular society rapid change has produced a reaction in nostalgia and a desire to recreate the past in certain ways. It is likely that this will have a liturgical counterpart – which may not be the same thing as living in the tradition of the Church. At present the Ecumenical Movement has slowed considerably, and many Churches show signs not only of renewed interest in, but also of renewed allegiance to, older denominational roots. Whatever the motivation, it is not impossible that, outwardly at least, the pendulum may begin to swing back.

Clearly, it would be possible to speculate at length on what forms the Liturgical Movement may take in the twenty-first century. The answer will be influenced and to some extent determined, humanly speaking, by other movements and shifts within the world Church. Yet, as the foregoing chapters suggest, it would be wrong to see the movement as no more than the product of other forces. It has had, and continues to have, its own rationale, force and inspiration. Perhaps the Liturgical Movement in the twentieth century will indeed come to be seen as the outward sign of God's reawakening of the Church.

Index

Abba, R. 38
Aland, K. 136
Albertine, R. 132n
Allen, H. T. 193
Ambrose, St 140
Andrewes, Bishop L. 38
Augustine, St 135
Aquinas, St Thomas 133

Ball, P. 141
Barth, K. 84, 136
Battifol, P. 19
Beauduin, L. 13, 23–5, 28, 30, 31, 37, 42, 43, 98, 109, 112, 187
Beckwith, R. T. 77
Benedict, St 18
Bennett, D. 107
Benoit, J.-D. 32
Billington, R. 89
Bishop, E. 30
Botte, B. 23, 29, 31, 34, 62, 66
Bouyer, L. 29, 66
Bowmer, J. C. 87n, 88
Boyd, M. 47–8
Bradshaw, P. F. 77, 172n
Brand, E. 192
Brock, C. 86
Brown, L. (Archbishop of Uganda; Bishop of St Edmundsbury and Ipswich), 55–8, 71, 72
Brunner, E. 136
Bucer, M. 183
Buchanan, C. O. viii, 53n, 74, 76, 78, 112, 118, 151n
Bugnini, A. 62, 63n, 66, 122n
Bulstrode, E. G. (Brother Edward) 45, 46
Burdon, A. 38n
Butterick, D. G. 193

Cabrol, F. 19, 31
Calvin, J. 81
Candole, H. de (Bishop of Knaresborough) viii, 43–8, 112, 123, 124
Capelle, B. 8, 31
Casel, O. 27–8, 31, 32, 188
Chrysostom, St John 96, 140
Chupungco, A. 158
Cicognano, Cardinal 62
Clark, H. H. 72
Clark, N. 124
Clerck, P. de 125, 126
Cockin, C. 119
Coleridge, S. T. 40
Connolly, R. H. 30
Cope, G. 76
Coquin, R. 19
Cosin, J. 150
Couratin, A. H. viii, 50, 85, 133
Cranmer, Archbishop T. 96, 149, 150
Crichton, J. D. 30, 63, 67
Cuming, G. J. viii, 76, 77, 172, 183

Cullmann, O. 136
Cyril of Jerusalem, St 140

Daniélou, J. 159
Davidson, Archbishop 43
Davies, H. 84, 85
Davies, J. G. 1n, 76, 195n, 196
Davies, M. 170n
Davies, R. 89
De Candole, H. (Bishop of Knaresborough) *see* Candole, H. de
De Clerck, P. *see* Clerk, P. de
De Puniet, P. *see* Puniet, P. de
Dean, S. 70
Deutsche, A. 187
Diekmann, G. 29, 188–9
Dix, G. 46, 49–50, 118, 127–8, 129, 138
Du Plessis, D. 107, 108
Dunlop, C. 51

Edwall, P. 37n
Ellard, G. 29, 34, 188
Engberding, H. 19
Erickson, C. D. 193

Farrar, A. 46, 49
Felici, Archbishop 63
Felix III, Pope 125
Fischer, B. 66
Fisher, J. D. C. 137n, 138
Fontaine, G. 122
Forsyth, P. T. 84
Frere, W. H. 41, 42, 43, 112
Frost, D. 119

Gaunt, A. 87
Gelasius, Pope 125
Gelineau, J. 66
George, R. 89, 124
Gibbons, S. 85
Gilmore, A. 91
Gore, C. 40
Gray, D. 40, 45n, 77
Gregory, J. 85
Gregory I, Pope 125
Gregory XVI, Pope 18
Grisbrooke, W. J. 38n, 100n
Guardini, R. 26n
Guéranger, P. L. P. vii, 17–20, 23
Gunton, C. 86
Gy, P. M. 66

Hardelen, A. 39n
Harper, M. 107, 108
Harrison, D. 92
Hatchett, M. 191
Hayman, E. 37n
Hebert, A. G. 43–6, 47, 49, 55, 112
Hellreigel, M. 188
Herwegen, I. 26–8, 31, 32, 37, 42, 45, 187, 188
Hippolytus 31, 56, 74, 85, 130, 172, 184
Holeton, D. 139n
Holmes, U. T. 191n
Holland, H. S. 40
Howell, C. 30
Hunter, J. 83
Huxtable, J. 84, 85, 86

Illingworth, J. R. 40

Jacob, C. K. 57
Jagger, P. 43n, 48n, 51
Jansen, C. 15
James, C. 77
James, P. D. (Baroness James of Holland Park) 78
Jasper, R. C. D. viii, 51, 71, 72–3, 75, 76, 90, 92
Jeremias, J. 136
Johanson, B. 86
John XXIII, Pope 61, 63, 97, 108
Jones, B. H. 190
Jones, D. 77
Jones, E. 30
Jounel, P. 66
Jubé, Abbé 15
Jungmann, J. 31, 62, 66, 188
Justin Martyr 74, 125

Kavanagh, A. 139, 140n
Keble, J. 39
Keene, J. 190
Keller, C. 57
Kennerly, K. V. 164
King, P. 183
Kingsley, C. 40
Klauser, T. 31, 62
Knox, J. 91
Koenker, E. B. 5n, 19, 21n, 24, 26, 167
Konstant, D. 126
King, H. 62–3

Ladd, W. P. 190
Lampe, G. W. 138, 139
Lang, C. 40
Laud, Archbishop W. 38
Leak, N. 83n
Leake, A. 152n
Leclercq, H. 31
Leenhardt, F.-J. 136
Lefèbvre, Archbishop vii, 167
Lengeling, E. 66
Lloyd, T. 77
Ludlow, J. M. 40
Lwakale, C. M. 163

Mabillon, J. 14
Marcel, P. C. 136
Marsh, J. 84
Marshall, M. 48
Martène, E. 14
Martimort, A.-G. 29, 66, 137
Martin, D. 168n, 170n
Mason, A. J. 138
Matthews, E. 70
Maurice, F. D. 40
Maxwell, J. R. 82n, 193
Maxwell, W. D. 37n
McArthur, A. 123
McElligott, B. 29
McHugh, H. 69
McKenna, J. H. 132n
McLaughlen, P. 46
McManus, F. 29, 188, 189
Michel, G. 127
Michel, V. 187–8
Micklem, N. 84, 175
Milner-White, E. 72
Mitchell, L. L. 191
Mocquereau, A. 18
Mohlberg, C. 31
Moll, W. E. 40
Moltmann, J. 166
Moreton, M. 77
Morhmann, C. 34
Mullen, P. 170n

Nagel, N. 192
Neale, J. M. 39
Neibuhr, H. R. 165
Newbigin, L. 57
Newman, J. H. 39
Newton, I. 16
Nickelsburg, G. W. E. 159n
Nicodemos the Hagiorite 100
Noel, C. 40
Notaras, M. 100

Orchard, W. E. 83
Owen, D. 86

Packard, K. 46
Parsch, P. 28, 187, 188
Parsons, E. L. 190
Paul VI, Pope 63, 140
Payne, E. A. 91
Perham, M. 77
Phillips, J. 84
Pius X, Pope vii, 23–4, 139
Pius XII, Pope 34
Pobee, J. S. 158, 162
Porter, H. B. 191
Pothier, J. 18
Puniet, P. de 183n
Pusey, E. 39
Puthanangady, P. 161

Quinn, F. 140

Ramsey, M. 73, 128
Ratcliff, E. C. 50, 76, 85, 131
Rattenbury, J. E. 87

Rattray, T. 38
Reinhold, H. A. 188, 189
Robinson, J. A. T. 50
Roguet, A.-M. 29, 137
Rose, H. J. 39
Routley, E. 86
Rowell, G. 78, 180n
Rupp, G. 90

Sainsbury, C. K. 72
Sanders, E. P. 121
Sarto, G. *see* Pius X, Pope
Sawyerr, H. 163n
Scales, D. A. 77
Schmemann, A. 101
Schnitker, T. 165
Seymour, W. J. 106
Shepherd, M. vii, 18, 32, 72, 190, 191
Silk, D. 78
Simon, U. 164, 165n.
Smalley, E. 91
Southcott, E. 47
Spinks, B. D. 50n, 77, 86, 128n, 131n, 164n, 165n
Stamoolis, J. 99
Stancliffe, D. 77
Stephens, E. 38
Stevenson, K. W. 50n, 77, 82n, 133n
Stillingfleet, E. 183
Suenens, Cardinal 109

Talbot, E. S. 40
Talley, T. J. 191
Tertullian 188
Thompson, D. 86
Thornton, L. S. 138
Timiades, E. 101
Tiller, J. E. 77
Todd, J. 84, 85
Tripp, D. 89
Tytler, D. 76

Vagaggini, C. 66
Vogel, C. 183n
Vorgrimler, H. 62, 65n

Wagner, J. 31, 66
Wainwright, G. 89, 90, 166
Wakefield, G. 89
Walker, M. 91
Walsh, C. 179
Ware, T. 99n
Webb, B. 39
Weil, L. 191
Wesley, J. 38, 39, 87, 106, 183
West, S. 190
White, J. F. 39n, 194
Whittaker, C. 76, 138
Wied, H. von 119, 126
Wigan, B. 51
Wilkerson, D. 107
William and Mary (King and Queen of England) 38
Willis, G. G. 51, 76, 77, 125
Wimber, J. vii, 109
Winward, S. F. 91, 176
Wolter, P. 20
Wybrew, H. 100n